Vegetarian *Homestyle* Cooking

A Guide to Heart-Healthy Lowfat Eating

Jeanne Tiberio, MS, RD

APPLETREE PRESS, INC.
Mankato, Minnesota

Appletree Press, Inc.
151 Good Counsel Drive, Suite 125
Mankato, MN 56001
Phone: (507) 345-4848 Fax: (507) 345-3002

This book is intended as a reference and cooking book only, not as a medical guide for self-treatment. The recipes given in this text were developed to help readers/cooks adopt a lowfat vegetarian eating pattern and are not intended as a substitute for any treatment prescribed by a physician.

CATALOGING-IN-PUBLICATION DATA

Tiberio, Jeanne, 1955-
    Vegetarian homestyle cooking: a guide to heart-healthy lowfat eating / by Jeanne Tiberio.
Mankato, MN: Appletree Press, Inc. ©1998.

256 p. : ill. ; 23 cm.

Includes index.

Summary: A homestyle collection of 175 easy-to-prepare, culturally-diverse vegetarian recipes that abound with heart-healthy, lowfat and cholesterol-free dishes to nourish the body and soul. Nutrient analysis and diabetic exchanges included.

ISBN 1-891011-00-6

1. Vegetarian cookery. 2. Low-fat diet—Recipes. 3. Low-cholesterol diet—Recipes. I. Title.

TX837   641.5/636   98-72722
                                                                                          CIP

Editor: Linda Hachfeld
Assistant editor: Samantha Massaglia
Graphic design & cover design: Sheila Chin Morris
Cover photograph: ©1998, Photodisc, Inc.

Printed in the United States of America

A c k n o w l e d g e m e n t s

The author wishes to express thanks to many people who provided assistance in this group effort.

I would like to specifically thank Kate Hammond, master chef of the Grapevine Restaurant in Salem, Mass., and Shelley Meyer (who makes and delivers vegetarian entrees to businesses) for their recipes. I feel fortunate to have worked with both of these great chefs.

Special thanks go out to the many patients I've seen who have supplied recipe ideas and given me feedback on my recipes. And special thanks to Harvey Zarren, MD who provided the inspiration to me and to so many others in his quest to promote preventative medicine.

I also appreciate the assistance of:
Sharon Basu
Christine Bobek
Eliza Bobek
Molly Bobek
Maureen Criasia
Karen Dipetro
Fran Tiberio
Peg Tiberio

The nutritional analysis of recipes was done with the Food Processor IV software package, Esha Corporation. The nutritional analysis for each recipe includes Diabetic Exchanges. These are based on the Diabetic Exchange List Guidelines updated in 1995 by the American Dietetic and the American Diabetes Associations. The Exchange List for Meal Planning is provided in *Appendix A.*

Contents

F o r e w o r d

One million Americans die each year from atherosclerosis, a vascular disease which has reached epidemic proportions in the United States. Atherosclerosis blocks arteries, causes heart attacks and strokes, and results in more deaths than all types of cancer combined. By age sixty, the average meat-eating American has processed about four tons of fat. Approximately seventy percent of thirteen-year old Americans already have atherosclerosis as a result of their diet. By age twenty, fifty-five percent of Americans have coronary disease; five percent of those have greater than seventy-five percent narrowing of at least one coronary artery.

Unfortunately, most Americans aren't aware that an estimated ninety percent of the deaths caused by atherosclerosis are preventable, primarily by diet. They aren't aware of the appropriate dietary role that the meat and dairy food groups should play, and consume excessive amounts of each. For example, the fat in nonskim dairy products and meat contribute to atherosclerosis. In addition, the animal protein in milk and meat can accelerate the growth of certain types of cancer cells so that they overcome the body's defenses.

Recent studies have shown that arteries are not just pipes. Rather, they open and close according to the demands of the areas to which they carry blood. These studies have led to new knowledge about the effects of diet on wellness. We now know that even one fatty meal can prevent appropriate opening of heart arteries for up to six hours in individuals who don't suffer from coronary disease. Patients with coronary disease may suffer the effects of one fatty meal for days. The resulting inability of arteries to open when more blood flow is needed often causes chest pain and clinical events leading to hospitalization.

It has been commonly known for years that plant-based diets (e.g. vegetarian diets) are much more conducive to good health than diets that include large amounts of meat and dairy products. A few members of the nutrition community have been courageous enough to promote and implement plant-based diets. Jeanne Tiberio, the author of *Vegetarian Homestyle Cooking* is one of those courageous, knowledgeable healthcare professionals. She has not altered the accuracy of her message because of the general perception that Americans aren't interested in changing their diet.

Jeanne accepted the reality that the American diet is the major cause of the common diseases, such as atherosclerosis. She also understands that nutrition is not a moral issue. Jeanne presents her knowledge and then works within parameters that her patients will accept. In designing her recipes, Jeanne has taken into account that people cannot and will not spend lots of time preparing foods.

Previously, Jeanne prepared a resource book introducing readers to vegetarianism. Building on that foundation, she has literally spent years producing this cookbook. The recipes have been carefully gathered and crafted. Jeanne has produced *Vegetarian Homestyle Cooking* with an enormous amount of knowledge and a love for her patients.

This book is the type of effort that must occur in order to stem the tide of diseases caused by nutritional extravagance that plague our country and that we are now exporting throughout the world. Thank you, Jeanne Tiberio for preparing this valuable cookbook for individuals seeking a better way of life!

Dr. Harvey Zarren M.D. F.A.C.C.
Medical Director
Cardiac Rehabilitation Center
AtlantiCare Medical Center
Lynn, Massachusetts

Introduction

I n my job as a nutritionist, I advise cardiac patients seeking to lower their cholesterol levels and weight through healthy methods. I designed this book for those who suffer from heart disease as well as those seeking preventative measures against high cholesterol and heart disease.

Research in the field of prevention and treatment of heart disease supports a lowfat vegetarian plan as an alternative therapy that is more effective than cholesterol-lowering medications or standard low-cholesterol diet plans. In an effort to provide further guidance for my patients, I met with cardiologist Dr. Harvey Zarren and discussed dietary guidelines that could enable patients to manage their cholesterol levels through diet alone. He felt that either the American Heart Association guidelines need to be more stringent, or that patients aren't adhering to the guidelines. In any case, patients aren't experiencing significant reductions in their cholesterol levels. Dr. Zarren maintained that dietary instruction should remain a critical part of the treatment regimen for cardiac patients. Recognizing that it takes a profound change in eating habits to achieve significant results, we have begun presenting the plan outlined in this book to our patients. We find that it yields significant improvement in cholesterol levels and weight loss while enabling patients to take responsibility for their own health.

It is important to keep in mind that a vegetarian diet represents a drastic change from the typical American diet. While preparing this book, I was concerned that many people might give up trying to switch to lowfat vegetarianism out of frustration. The changes can be difficult, given that the tastes and habits of many Americans are of the "meat and potatoes" variety. Successfully altering our eating habits means committing to change. In other words, simply being told what to eat is not enough. Anyone who has lost weight only to gain it all back knows that it is difficult to leave comfortable habits behind. We need to be psychologically prepared to make changes without feeling deprived.

Transitioning to a new eating plan requires change on several levels. I've discovered that simply describing which foods to avoid on a vegetarian diet doesn't provide a complete picture of what must be done. A complete change requires learning what to eat as well as the practicalities of making changes happen. This is especially true for those attempting to significantly reduce their cholesterol intake by removing all meat, chicken and fish from their diet. The piece of meat is no longer the centerpiece of the meal with other foods playing supporting roles. In fact, a few of my patients reported to me that their dinner plate consisted of a potato, a vegetable and a blank space or "void" where the meat once was. Other members of the family had slabs of meat in that space and my patients felt unsatisfied and deprived, with good reason. The goal here is to begin viewing grains as the centerpiece of a nutritious American diet and to shift to a diet higher in complex carbohydrates and lower in fat.

I had originally planned these recipes for cardiac patients who elected to start a lowfat vegetarian eating plan. However, since a lowfat vegetarian plan results in weight loss, it is likely that it would also combat hypertension, diabetes, obesity, and perhaps cancer. Taking preventative measures to preserve your health is well worth the effort.

As a 48-year old male patient lamented,

"I didn't start thinking about what I ate until I had chest pain. I wish I had learned to eat better a long time ago so I could have avoided this scare and worry. Suddenly, I was a very sick person having to undergo all these painful tests."

I encourage you to remember that it's never too late to begin making healthy changes to your lifestyle. As you develop a personal repertoire of lowfat vegetarian recipes, you will experience the satisfaction that accompanies healthful eating and the enjoyment that accompanies delicious vegetarian food.

As a 52-year old female patient happily explained,

"At first I thought I couldn't do this, but I'm losing weight without starving myself. Now, I'm excited about trying new recipes and I want to learn more about it."

Jeanne Tiberio, MS, RD
Author

Chapter 1

Making the Case for a Vegetarian Diet

I f you are struggling to lower your cholesterol level or to drop a few pounds, you are not alone. The realization that what we eat directly affects our health is now acknowledged by both clinicians and the general public. The medical community recognizes that it needs to pay attention to patients' eating habits as part of a total preventative program. Many health professionals now take an assertive approach, educating people on the benefits of a lowfat vegetarian eating plan. This book is designed to assist those who wish to aggressively pursue such a lifestyle and improve their chances for a disease-free life.

Making significant lifestyle changes can be daunting, even though you may be aware that they are important for your well-being. As a nutritionist, it has been my job for many years to help people overcome obstacles that prevent change. If you wish to undertake an eating plan that enhances long-term health and vitality, this book can help you. The recipes in *Vegetarian Homestyle Cooking* are easy to prepare and use familiar ingredients. Tasty, wholesome food is the enjoyable reward that accompanies a vegetarian lifestyle.

A Brief Introduction to Vegetarianism

When did the modern vegetarian movement begin?
Although literature on vegetarianism was first published in ancient Greece, the modern vegetarian movement actually began in1847, in Great Britain, with the formation of The Vegetarian Society. Shortly after that, the first issue of *The Vegetarian Messenger*, a monthly periodical devoted to vegetarianism was

published in 1849. Since then, the vegetarian movement has experienced consistent, widespread growth. Vegetarian societies exist in virtually every nation, and the global vegetarian community constantly works to establish ties among its various factions. (see page 239, *Suggested Readings and Web sites*)

Until the 1970s, the questions asked by the nutrition community were fairly straight-forward: Are Americans getting enough nutrients? The focus was on preventing deficiency diseases caused by inadequate protein, vitamins and minerals. National surveys in the late 1940s indicated that Americans were consuming the same number of calories as we are today, but more calories were coming from complex carbohydrates and fewer were coming from fat.

In the 1970s, the relationship between eating a high-fiber, lowfat diet and the prevention of heart disease became clear. The American vegetarian movement had begun. Eating too much meat and other high-fat foods was now associated with ill-health.

What has happened recently?

Times have changed. Most Americans have access to a broad spectrum of foods, and protein malnutrition is rare, while heart disease has become the leading cause of death in the United States. Until recently, it was also generally assumed that the typical American could not adjust to a vegetarian diet. That assumption is being tested as people of all ages are increasing the number of vegetarian meals in their diet.

Increased media focus has caused many people to assume that merely limiting meat consumption will produce the desired change in their cholesterol level. While the typical American diet derives approximately 32.8[1] percent of its calories from fat, much of which is found in meat, it is important to note that our per capita intake of regular cheeses has also increased over the past several years. In addition, frequently eaten snack foods high in saturated fat can contribute to increased levels of total blood cholesterol and body weight.

Recognizing the need for further dietary information, the United States government and the American Heart Association (AHA) have published guidelines for healthy eating that emphasize whole grains and produce and limit fat from all sources (see *Appendix A*). The current AHA guidelines suggest that no more than 30 percent of our daily calories come from fat. By significantly limiting meat intake and exercising frequently, many Americans reduce their

---

[1] 1994 Survey of food intakes by individuals, compiled by USDA, Riverdale, MD.

total blood cholesterol levels to 150 to 200 mg/dl. However, our eating habits may need to be further adjusted in order to achieve our goals.

What does current research tell us?

During the past two decades, nutritionists have studied groups that practice vegetarianism. For example, members of the Seventh Day Adventists (a religious group that advocates vegetarianism) experience heart disease less frequently and have lower cholesterol levels.[2] Members who are vegans (vegetarians who exclude all meat and dairy products from their diet) have the lowest cholesterol levels and less heart disease.

The work of Dr. Dean Ornish[3] offers a revolutionary solution to the growing problem of high cholesterol and heart disease. Basically, Dr. Ornish suggests that symptomatic heart disease can be prevented, and even reversed by following a lowfat vegetarian diet and using effective stress management techniques. This exciting news opens the door for further research on the effects of nutrition and stress in heart disease prevention.

The Ornish plan allows 10 percent of a patient's daily calories to come from fat. It restricts intake of all animal products (including chicken, fish and dairy) with the exception of some skim milk, yogurt and egg white. Stress reduction techniques, such as yoga, meditation and group therapy are also included in the program. The entire program has been dramatically successful at lowering weight and cholesterol.

Yet, the Ornish plan raises a few questions as well. For instance, if you aim for 10 percent of your calories to come from fat, and you actually get 20 (a more realistic assumption for the average American) can you lower your cholesterol and weight enough to achieve the benefits you desire? What roles do relaxation techniques and group therapy play? Can stress, by itself, be a stronger risk factor for heart disease and cancer than we previously assumed? What about the contribution of exercise? For example, if you exercise four times a week for 30 minutes, can you choose a diet that allows more than 10 percent of its calories from fat and still receive the same health benefits?

---

[2] Fraser, G.E. "Determinants of ischemic heart disease in 7th Day Adventists: A review." *American Journal of Clinical Nutrition.* 1988, 48 (supplement) 833-836.

[3] Gould, K.L., Ornish, D. et al. "Changes in myocardial perfusion abnormalities by positron emission tomography after long term intense risk factor modification." *JAMA.* 1995, 274:894-901.

The answer is neither simple nor universal. There is no single number of fat grams appropriate for every individual. The same can be said of exercise programs and stress reduction techniques. Currently, nutritionists advise patients to eat liberal amounts of some foods and to cut back on others. Patients constantly ask them to define the word "moderation," and the responses they receive vary. However, nutritionists do seem to agree on one point: There is no one set of guidelines that will work for everyone. Yet, the need for a diet low in saturated fat is universal. Nutritionists also agree that many Americans derive most of their saturated fat intake from meats and dairy products.

Other Possible Health Benefits From Vegetarianism

Individuals with hypertension can lower their blood pressure by losing weight and lowering their sodium intake through a lowfat vegetarian plan.[4] Foods like crackers, chips, bakery foods and fast foods contain large amounts of salt and fat. Cutting down on them can dramatically reduce salt intake. A lowfat vegetarian plan like the one I am proposing would eliminate or greatly reduce the amount of these foods included in the diet.

For individuals suffering from adult onset diabetes, the emphasis has shifted from the importance of removing sugar from the diet to establishing weight maintenance with a lowfat, controlled-carbohydrate dietary plan. Scientists studied overweight diabetics who achieved a realistic weight range and whose blood sugar levels subsequently dropped. Lowering their blood sugar enables diabetics to control diabetes and avoid the serious side-effects of the disease.

For those who wish to reduce their risk of cancer or prevent a recurrence of the illness, a lowfat vegetarian plan followed to any extent could be beneficial. It is rarely disputed that switching from a diet high in saturated fats to one that includes large amounts of fruits, vegetables and whole grains can reduce your risk of cancer. This type of eating plan should also encourage a good intake of beta-carotene (from vegetables) and soy protein. Although not yet proven in human studies, recent studies of animals suggest a link between higher consumption of these items and lower rates of certain cancers.[5]

[4] Beilin, L.J. "Vegetarian and other complex diets, fats, fiber, and hypertension." *American Journal of Clinical Nutrition.* 1994, 59 (supplement):1130-1135.

[5] Thorogood, M., Man, J, & Appleby, P. "Risk of death from cancer and ischemic heart disease in meat and non-meat eaters." *BMJ.* 1994, 308 (6945): 1667-1670.

Are all vegetarians the same?

Numerous approaches to vegetarianism exist. The following is a description of various types of vegetarianism. However, it is by no means a complete list. Many different schools of vegetarianism continue to evolve:

❖ **semi- and demi-vegetarianism**—partial vegetarianism. Adherents eat fish as well as broad-based plant foods.
❖ **lacto-ovo vegetarianism**—adherents do not eat red meat, poultry, fish or seafood. Instead, their diet consists of broad-based plant foods, milk, cheese, yogurt and eggs.
❖ **lacto-vegetarianism**—lacto-vegetarians also eat broad-based plant foods, milk, cheese and yogurt; however, they do not consume eggs.
❖ **vegan-vegetarianism**—adherents are strict vegetarians who eat broad-based plant foods but exclude all dairy products and eggs from their diets. Essentially, all commercial snack foods, pastries and desserts are restricted.

Making the Transition to Vegetarianism

How do we begin?

If a lifestyle change can be reduced to a simple set of instructions, and if research suggests that vegans have the best success in preventing heart disease, it might seem logical to advocate a strict vegan plan for everyone. However, the main obstacle to such an approach may be the feasibility for all Americans of adopting a strict vegan regime.

In order to meet the RDA (Recommended Daily Allowance) of 50 grams of protein per day, we need to eat tofu/soy products and beans every day. Many of the patients I see cannot tolerate, or are unwilling to include these foods daily, especially right from the start. Nuts and seeds contain too much fat for daily use. Even skim milk, egg substitutes and fat-free cheese would be eliminated. That leaves most Americans with limited choices, especially in restaurants.

It is no surprise, then, that one patient stated,

"I didn't see anything vegetarian on the menu, so I just got the prime rib with the fries."

This person didn't realize that other options, such as the baked fish were an acceptable choice. Thus, I recommend that my patients begin by eliminating all meat from their diet and follow a broad-based vegetarian plan (including skim milk, fat-free cheese and yogurt, egg substitutes, and fish, as necessary). They are usually successful with this less rigid approach.

What's the next step?

In my opinion, most of us resist change that we realize will be beneficial because we fear that it will also be unpleasant. The perception that lowfat foods are not satisfying is being challenged as recent advancements in food technology and preparation are helping to make lowfat vegetarian foods easy to prepare and delicious to eat. If you want to make permanent changes in your diet, there are a few interrelated societal factors to consider.

First, what we think of as our food preferences are actually the eating habits we acquired during childhood. We became accustomed to meals centered around meat that perhaps ended with a high-fat dessert. As with other habits, we usually have to work to change them. In addition, the decrease in work-related physical activity and increase in car travel over the past 40 years have lessened the need for total fat calories. To make matters worse, television advertisers use manipulative words like creamy and sizzling to tell us how much we like the taste of fat. That creates a conflict—we need to restrict these tempting foods that are constantly being paraded in front of our eyes.

There is another issue that may be just as important as recognizing our ingrained eating habits: the amount of stress in our lives. The type of stress experienced today is different than that experienced 10, 20, or even 50 years ago. Instead of physical stresses, such as being uncomfortably cold in winter, the stresses of the modern world seem to have changed. Today's stress seems to lead to feelings of frustration and isolation. We sometimes use food to soothe our nerves or to act as a single affordable pleasure. Although it has become widely recognized that over-eating does not reduce stress and it definitely leads to obesity, heart disease and diabetes, we continue to over-eat.

Reducing saturated fat and cholesterol requires making an effort to change. The one common trait that I see in people who are successful is a strong belief or confidence in their ability to make these changes. The focus of their attention is not on the foods they are giving up, but on their self-improvement. They often manage to eliminate the link between negative emotions and craving fattening foods. When I facilitate vegetarian support groups, I enjoy watching members give each other encouragement and helpful advice. One member may be a vegan vegetarian while another eats chicken and occasionally red meat. But they all choose to be there because they want to adopt healthier eating habits. *Chapter 2* provides information about how to make these changes achievable for you.

So, what's the best diet for everyone?

It appears that no individual set of guidelines or a specific diet plan will work for everyone. Generally, we have evolved to the recommendations for a lowfat diet that focuses on reducing both saturated fat and dietary cholesterol. The eating plan that I recommend most frequently is meatless and low in fat. (see *Appendix B: Vegetarian Food Guide Pyramid* and *Appendix C: 14-Days of Sample Lowfat Vegetarian Menus*) The recipes and meal plans that I developed result in a diet plan ranging from 10 to 15 percent of total calories from fat, if followed faithfully. However, it is important to focus on the cholesterol, weight, blood pressure, or blood sugar levels that you want to achieve.

I firmly believe that the benefits of adopting a lowfat vegetarian regime exceed the difficulty in adjusting to a lifestyle change. The collection of recipes in *Vegetarian Homestyle Cooking* is both vegetarian and very low in saturated fat. They are designed to help you make a variety of meals that will convince you and your family to eat well.

Chapter 2

The Relationship Between What We Eat
And How We Feel

Once you acknowledge the need to improve your eating habits, what should you do next? I believe that it is crucial to understand the emotional importance that we delegate to certain foods that we are reluctant to eliminate from our diet. In other words, it is sometimes hard to remove some foods from our diet because we have an emotional attachment to them. Unfortunately, our relationship to high-calorie, high-fat foods is paradoxical. While we find such foods appealing before eating them, most of us experience feelings of guilt afterward because high-calorie, high-fat foods do nothing to improve our health or meet our cholesterol and weight goals. In fact, they may be damaging to our health. This chapter offers some advice about severing the link between emotions and over-eating.

The Link Between Emotions and Over-Eating

It is quite normal to find certain foods satisfying or even soothing at times. We associate many foods with important events in our lives (holidays, graduations) and with rewards for good behavior. Conversely, foods found on a strict low-calorie diet (i.e., lettuce, grapefruit) are associated with punishment for letting our cholesterol or weight get out of control. High-fat foods can become a soothing balm that helps us through the daily stresses of our lives, and our reliance on them can become so subtle that we don't recognize the association.

Often, incidental stresses, like a traffic jam or an argument at work can lead to stress overload. Later that day, we may find ourselves craving a cheese-steak sandwich or ice cream, even though the connection with the earlier stressful event is not obvious. Cravings for high-fat foods can be in response to a variety of emotions ranging from anxiety and depression to boredom or even anger. The intensity of emotions triggered by eating what we perceive to be a "bad" food can actually raise the level of importance that a food has for us.

A direct link also exists between foods that we crave and foods that we feel are "forbidden," as anyone who has been on a strict diet can appreciate. For example, patients on kidney dialysis have to restrict their fruit and vegetable intake to limit their potassium. They report craving oranges and bananas that they normally wouldn't consider a treat. This perceived deprivation sets up a cycle of guilt and feelings of failure that affects their attitude toward these foods.

Social pressure and personal relationships play a central role in determining our eating habits, both at home and in public. During a nutrition counseling session, I was trying to convince a woman to stop buying ice cream to store in her freezer and I clearly lost the battle of wills. She said that she had to buy 2 half gallons of ice cream a week because her husband ate some every night.

I asked, "Are there any flavors that he likes but you don't?"

"None," she replied, "we both have the same specific tastes. We like everything."

Her decision to accommodate her husband's preferences undermined her efforts to change and provided her with a rationalization for continuing to eat ice cream.

Similarly, when we are at a Chinese restaurant with friends, and the pu-pu platter has already been ordered, it's easier to say nothing than ask someone to share a vegetarian entrée. In these subtle ways, we postpone making choices that help us meet our cholesterol and weight goals.

Clever advertising also affects our perception of how to effectively control our eating habits. Advertising campaigns often contain slogans that suggest you can eat unlimited high-calorie foods without gaining an ounce. This helps reinforce the myth that foods will not taste good to us unless they contain a lot of fat. Advertisers of diet products encourage us to fantasize that permanent weight loss is easy to achieve when common sense and experience tell us otherwise.

Many of the original vegetarian recipes developed during the vegetarian movement two decades ago were high in cream, cheese and eggs because chefs assumed that Americans wouldn't find lowfat foods satisfying. While it is true that fat helps to blend spices and improves the texture of a food, it is also true that a little fat goes a long way.

The concept of moderation also plays a key role in a successful lowfat vegetarian plan. Eating should be an enjoyable experience, and you can eat rich foods occasionally. For instance, a piece of cake at a party or a slice of garlic bread at a restaurant will not have a major impact on your total fat intake for the week. However, eating a large volume of such foods on a regular basis can create problems. Then, once an elevated cholesterol or progressive heart disease has occurred, it takes a very lowfat diet to help us recover our health.

How Do I Modify My Behavior to Modify My Food Choices?

A growing number of people are starting to look at the big picture and ask, "How can we teach ourselves to eat healthy foods throughout our lives so we can prevent premature heart disease and obesity?" We're beginning to realize that happier people eat healthier and eating healthy foods makes us feel better about ourselves. Many of us may wonder how we can teach ourselves to eat healthy foods and enjoy them. As with any other change, eating healthy foods becomes easier over time and can eventually become an habitual behavior. In other words, as we change our psychological perception of what tastes good, we might begin to instinctively avoid fried foods and meats, and opt instead for lowfat vegetarian foods.

If an effortless approach to improving eating habits exists, I've yet to hear of it. While it is fairly easy to decide to avoid circumstances that make lowfat vegetarian eating difficult, we need to look beyond simple logistics and into our rational for choosing the foods we eat. It might seem natural for us to simply embark on a program that calls for eliminating meat and fatty foods if the result is a leaner, healthier body. But many reasons why it might not work can surface, bringing us back to the issue of stress. An increase in stress often inhibits people from making positive changes in their lives. Thus, a change in eating habits should include a plan to manage stress and help us feel more relaxed.

Consider that foods aren't inherently good or bad. Perhaps what we really object to is being asked to change. We need to change not only the foods themselves, but also our perception of what is satisfying food. Making lasting changes requires incentive, confidence, and the belief that our efforts will reward us with improved health.

We need to sever the connection between what we eat and how we feel about ourselves. Healthy foods should be satisfying and eating can be an enjoyable experience without the high-fat content when we're not feeding our emotions. Only then can we more easily tune into our hunger/satiety cues and make healthier food choices. It will make the task of switching to a lowfat eating plan more of a natural transition.

Recommendations for Transitioning to Lowfat, Vegetarian Eating

1. Talk to people who have been successful at improving their eating habits. Ask them to describe, in detail, what has worked for them. This exchange can take place with family members and friends or can be facilitated through participation in a peer support group. Consult your physician or registered dietitian about the availability of nutrition support groups in your area. In my experience, even the most reluctant patient is buoyed by the nonjudgmental support of other individuals in similar circumstances.

2. Adopt a stress management technique or activity. This can be anything you feel comfortable with and can do daily. Stress reduction techniques such as yoga, meditation, guided imagery tapes, or deep breathing exercises usually work well. You could also participate in more traditional activities like listening to classical music or joining a therapy group.

3. Engage in physical exercise to reduce stress and burn calories. I recommend combining some form of physical activity 4 or 5 times a week in combination with a daily relaxation activity. Try to find 2 or 3 different physical exercises that you can do frequently. Choose at least one activity that can be performed indoors, so you don't have to forego exercise during poor weather.

4. Record your food intake for 3 days, including all snacks you've eaten. Study it and ask yourself the following questions:

   ❖ Are there certain times when I binge on high-fat foods?

   ❖ In particular, are most of my high-fat foods consumed after 5 p.m.?

   ❖ If so, what outside pressures influence this behavior.?

5. Set realistic goals for your cholesterol level, weight loss or whatever change you wish to accomplish by switching to a lowfat vegetarian eating plan. No particular timetable or degree of change is right for everyone. Choose what works best for you.

6. Try to make the distinction between physiological hunger and the desire for food. It normally takes 3 to 4 hours for a meal to entirely leave our stomach. (Digestion time may be shorter if the meal is small or very low in fat.) A small snack between each meal and before bedtime is encouraged to control dinner portions and avoid hunger.

7. Plan ahead to have healthy snacks available throughout the day. Include starchy snacks such as cereals and lowfat crackers. If you're craving a high-fat snack after you've eaten, delay doing something about it and try to divert your attention to another activity. If you feel the need to have high-fat snacks around the house during your transition period, keep them on high shelves or at the bottom of the freezer.

8. Experiment with different types of vegetarian foods and learn what appeals to you in both taste and texture. Do not force yourself to eat foods that you really don't like. Develop a list of vegetarian recipes that you can look forward to eating on a regular basis.

9. Don't reward yourself with a high-fat meal after a period of lowfat eating. It sends your mind mixed signals; we want to break the link between high-fat foods and emotional satisfaction.

10. Think about the accomplishments that you have achieved thus far in your life. Whether it is maintaining a long-term relationship, raising children, completing a difficult job, winning a race, getting a college degree—all of these accomplishments have one thing in common: they have all required effort and we inherently know this. Keeping our bodies in good physical condition should be no different. Exercise, weight control, healthy eating habits, and stress reduction do require some effort and discipline, but the reward is worth the effort.

A Final Reminder About Dietary Changes

Recognizing that we often associate our favorite foods with a sense of emotional well-being is an important step toward improving our eating habits. Eating should be a positive experience and healthy foods should taste good enough to tempt us to try them again. I believe that eating vegetarian foods can both enhance dining enjoyment and improve our health. After all, it only makes sense that healthy foods should give us contentment and pleasure.

Chapter 3

Questions and Answers About "Going Vegetarian"

When I advise people about switching to a lowfat eating plan, they often ask important questions about the rationale for becoming a vegetarian. I've compiled the following sampling of questions and answers to help alleviate any doubts or confusion about the value and purpose of "going vegetarian".

I am willing to try these vegetarian meals, but I need to feed my family as well. How can I convince them to join me?

This is a difficult question, as every household consists of persons with individual needs and preferences. If you live and share food with others, switching to vegetarian meals, even part time, will likely have some impact on their eating behavior as well. One way to approach this is to see it as a family endeavor that will benefit everyone in the household. Also, by helping the younger members of your household become accustomed to lowfat eating, you are helping to establish a healthy lifelong pattern. Children who avoid a high-fat diet from an early age, and see their parents doing the same, have a much better chance of maintaining good eating habits and normal weight as adults. Children and adults who maintain a lower fat, high fiber intake may reduce their risk of developing heart disease and certain cancers as well.

What if the others in my household still aren't convinced to try lowfat vegetarian foods?

If the "it's good for everyone" argument won't convince them, try telling the adults in your household that switching to a lowfat vegetarian plan is something that you need to do for yourself to improve your health. In other words, forge ahead and prepare your own meals and hope that the others in the household will begin trying some of the new recipes. A gradual approach may work well in this circumstance. It's important to allow your family time to adjust to your new lifestyle. You can start by serving different types of vegetarian dishes once or twice a week rather than all at once. Try serving old favorites like pasta and pizza, made with vegetarian and lowfat ingredients. Include a few cookie or other dessert recipes. In other words, demonstrate that vegetarianism is more than eating cooked vegetables.

If I start working on my vegetarian diet today, how soon will I see my cholesterol level go down?

This question gives me an opportunity to discuss the importance of seeing a lowfat eating plan as a lifelong improvement in eating behavior rather than a temporary diet. Although it is only natural to seek immediate results, we should first consider two things:

On a physical level, the cholesterol numbers could drop a few months after starting a lowfat vegetarian diet. However, the lower cholesterol level will only result in a lowered risk of heart disease if it is sustained. You must continue on a dietary regime long-term to keep the cholesterol down and reap the long-term benefits.

It is psychologically uplifting to see an improvement in our cholesterol numbers after a few months on a lowfat dietary regime. This may be followed by a feeling of relief and then a return to the previous poor eating habits. It takes some patience and diligence to turn significant changes into permanent new eating habits; therefore, although the goal here is lowfat vegetarianism, it doesn't have to happen over night. Start by eliminating foods with the highest fat content from your diet, then move ahead in your pursuit of long-term lowfat vegetarian eating.

Should I be measuring how much fat is in my diet?

The prevailing wisdom of experts in the field of nutrition is that a combination of reducing fat and increasing physical activity should help you reduce weight and lower blood cholesterol. A reduction in fat usually results in fewer total calories, even if you're consuming more carbohydrates, because fat is a very dense form of calories. At 9 calories per gram (vs. approximately 4 calories per gram for protein and carbohydrates), fat is by far the calorie culprit in food.

If you want to analyze your intake of calories and fat, follow the instructions below:

1. Purchase a calorie and fat counter at your local bookstore.

2. Record everything you eat and drink for 3 or more days, leaving space in the right margin to list calories and fat content for each item. Remember to include portions of everything you eat, including additional fats that you add, such as margarine. Be honest with yourself! The effort is not worth much otherwise.

3. Next to each item, record calories and fat grams from your calorie book in 2 separate columns.

4. Add the calorie and fat grams in the columns. Divide by the number of days.

5. Multiply the total daily grams of fat by 9. The total is your fat calories.

6. Divide your fat calorie total from above into your total calories. Then multiply by 100 to get the percentage of total calories from fat.

Hint: A registered dietitian at your local hospital or medical clinic can also help you calculate your percentage of total calories from fat. You can also purchase a computer program that provides a complete nutritional analysis of your intake. Your goal should be to get less than 20 percent of your calories from fat and to be as close as possible to 10 percent.

I experience cravings for meat once or twice a week. Won't these cravings get worse if I try to give up meat altogether?

Yes, you may crave meat once in a while after giving it up. Although irritating, the feelings will be temporary as you focus your thoughts on other things. Individual cravings for certain foods under specific conditions are well documented but not well understood. Obvious habitual cravings diminish when the habit of eating certain foods is broken. For example, if you eat a candy bar every workday at 3 p.m., you shouldn't be surprised to suddenly crave something chocolate at 3 p.m. on Saturday.

Other types of cravings, such as those experienced by pregnant women, cannot be tied to habit or usual preferences. Whether or not there is a biochemical as well as psychological basis for all cravings remains a mystery. But it is reasonable to say that a craving for red meat is not a signal that your body needs something that only red meat provides.

I've heard that some people are "partial vegetarians" who include chicken in their lowfat diet. Is there any reason why it wouldn't be advisable to eat chicken on a vegetarian diet?

It's your choice as the extent to which you want to include vegetarian dishes in your meal plan. Recent theory suggests that if you want to prevent heart disease (or halt its progression if you already suffer from it), it's a good idea to limit fat from all sources and omit all animal products. All red meat, chicken and fish contain some saturated fat and cholesterol (even skinless chicken breasts). Of the 3 choices, fish is the lowest in saturated fat and contains the type of fatty acids that can raise your level of HDL cholesterol, the good cholesterol fragment.

Foods of plant origin (such as grains, fruits and vegetables) have no cholesterol and only trace amounts of saturated fat. A lowfat vegetarian program ensures a reduction in cholesterol and probably weight as well. Your personal goal for your cholesterol level may depend on whether you already have heart disease. If you haven't done so already, you should have your cholesterol checked and discuss your goal numbers with your physician.

Is my cholesterol so high because I am genetically predisposed to having high cholesterol?

We all make cholesterol in our livers and would do just fine if we took in no additional cholesterol from foods after age two. Recent evidence suggests that only 1 out of 500 people have "defective genes"[1] that cause their liver to make too much cholesterol. The rest of us have high cholesterol levels due to lifestyle factors. Thus, the optimal dietary plan for all of us includes foods low in both cholesterol and saturated fat.

---

[1] The First International Symposium on Multiple Risk Factors in Cardiovascular Disease sponsored by NIH and National Heart, Lung and Blood Institute; Phoenix, AZ; October, 1991.

If cholesterol in foods only comes from animal sources, what's wrong with the fat found in vegetable products like margarine and potato chips?

Foods high in saturated fat, even if they're cholesterol-free, can result in your body producing additional cholesterol. When a large amount of fat, especially saturated fat, enters the blood stream at one time, it can adhere to the walls of the arteries. In addition, recent evidence suggests that the saturated fat may be blocking the control of cholesterol synthesis in the liver.[2] Your liver then continues to make cholesterol and send it into your bloodstream, even though it is not needed.

Many common foods, like stick margarine, contain no cholesterol but are high in saturated fat. In order to produce a stick of margarine, the vegetable fatty acids must be hardened or "saturated." This change in molecular structure is called "trans" configuration. Trans fatty acids can elevate total and LDL cholesterol levels. Fried snacks (i.e., potato chips, snack crackers) and pastries can sabotage anyone's effort to control cholesterol and weight and should be avoided as much as possible. Trans fatty acids are used to increase the shelf life of these products. Thus, a dietary plan that is low in both saturated fat and cholesterol reduces the amount of cholesterol made by our liver, and will result in the most dramatic improvement.

So, what should a cholesterol-conscious snacker choose?

Any lowfat, easy-to-handle food can be used as a snack. When asked which healthy snacks they enjoy, people often mention fresh fruit, but hesitate to mention starchy foods. Yet, whole-grain, complex carbohydrate foods like breadsticks, cereal and popcorn also make excellent snacks.

I suggest checking labels for fat on processed snacks and frozen desserts. Bulk items like crackers and frozen yogurt in half gallon containers are more difficult to eat in smaller amounts. The portions recommended are unrealistic for most appetites, and the fat adds up when you are eating 4 or 5 times the recommended portions. Try fat-free frozen items on a stick, or cracker-type products with 1 or 0 grams of fat per serving.

Remember, there is no reason to feel guilty about snacking. In fact, eating 3 meals a day along with small snacks is a more natural way to feed the body.

[2] Brown, M.S. & Goldstein, J.L. "How LDL receptors influence cholesterol and atherosclerosis." *Scientific American. 1984, 251*: 58-66.

Afternoon snacks can cut down on portion overload at night, when most fat calories are consumed.

Can I get enough protein if I become a strict vegetarian?

Yes, because all foods, excluding fruit and fat contain protein. Aside from the elderly, acutely ill, or the very poor, most Americans get plenty of protein. The recommended protein intake varies with each individual, but 50 grams of protein per day is adequate for most healthy adults. The average American typically eats twice that amount of protein.

The American Dietetic Association (ADA) put its stamp of approval on vegetarian diets supplying adequate amounts of protein. In its 1997 position statement, ADA states, "Appropriately planned vegetarian diets are healthful, are nutritionally adequate, and provide health benefits in the prevention and treatment of certain diseases."[3]

It was once thought that plant-based proteins were incomplete or of lower quality than protein from animal products because plants lacked all eight amino acids. That belief was based on research done decades ago and called for various plant-based foods to be eaten together at the same meal to provide complete protein. You may still see vegetarian books asking the reader to combine beans and rice or beans and corn to maximize amino acids.

Research today suggests that complementary plant proteins do not need to be consumed at the same time. Plant foods contain all essential amino acids, just in varied amounts. If you eat a wide variety of plant foods (i.e., beans or tofu, rice, pasta, bread, potatoes) over the course of a day and get enough food to meet your energy needs, you can be confident that you will receive the adequate amount and type of protein your body needs. Nuts, seeds, legumes, tofu and soy milk are all high in protein. Other vegetables plus breads and cereals supply somewhat less but are still good sources.

The sample menus in *Appendix C* provide examples of full day menus that provide more than adequate amounts of protein when using the recipes from *Vegetarian Homestyle Cooking*.

---

[3] American Dietetic Association, "Position of the American Dietetic Association: Vegetarian diets." *JADA*. 1997, 11:1317-1321.

I'm trying to find lowfat substitutions for protein, but I noticed that tofu has some fat in it and peanut butter has even more. Should I limit my consumption of these products?

It is true that tofu and peanut butter contain some fat. However, they are relatively low in saturated fat and contain no cholesterol. The issue here is both the type of fat and the amount normally eaten. For example, the average serving of tofu is 4 ounces and contains about 6 grams of fat. You would have to eat a pound of tofu to get an equivalent number of fat grams as the typical 2-ounce portion of whole-milk cheese. The cheese also contains saturated fat, which is absent in the tofu.

Peanut butter is a little different than tofu. While it is a plant-based source of protein, it does have a higher percentage of fat. Therefore, if you're interested in losing weight, you will need to limit the portion size; 2 tablespoons is a typical portion. Both tofu and peanut butter are sold in reduced-fat versions.

Remember that Americans take in much of their fat from animal products, high-fat desserts and snacks. If you eliminate these from your diet, you can certainly enjoy a little peanut butter now and then.

What are some habits to watch out for now that I am committed to lowering my cholesterol and losing some weight?

Here are 3 habits that come up frequently in my discussions with patients about their diet histories. Each of these habits undermines patients' sincere efforts to make dietary changes:

Eating out too much. This includes fast food restaurants, sandwich shops and eating at friends' homes. In other words, anywhere you have not prepared the food and have limited the amount of added fat. It can be difficult to find a lowfat vegetarian meal in most restaurants; therefore, you need to treat eating out as the exception, not the rule.

Not eating enough during the day in an effort to reduce your calories. I find that for my patients, skipping breakfast undermines their ability to control calories. Eating regular meals such as breakfast and lunch promotes a sense of well-being and keeps the appetite at bay until the next meal. When you skimp on calories during the day, you will almost inevitably overeat at night. Consume the majority of your calories while you are still active during the day so they are less likely to be stored as fat.

Having an unrealistic idea of portion size. We all have a tendency to underestimate how much we're eating. The idea of limiting our portions might make us anxious. I tell my patients the opposite of what their parents may have told them: try not to clean your plate. Chances are, you have eaten enough before your plate is completely empty. It may seem wasteful, but if you eat more than you need, your body will not utilize the nutrients and will store the calories as fat. If you are not full after a meal, you can look forward to a cup of herbal tea, decaf coffee or a piece of fresh fruit.

I read an article that suggested checking homosysteine as well as cholesterol levels in the body. What is homocysteine and what is it's connection to heart disease?

Homocysteine is a naturally occurring substance that is a by-product of amino acid metabolism. (Amino acids are the building blocks or proteins that we eat, which need to be converted, or metabolized into new proteins for our body). When homocysteine is produced, folic acid is needed to convert homocysteine to another amino acid. Recent evidence demonstrates that an inadequate intake of folic acid results in elevated levels of homocysteine in the bloodstream.

Elevated homocysteine levels are now considered by some to be an independent risk factor for cardiovascular disease. It is theorized that homocysteine plays a role in the buildup of plaque on the walls of the artery, leading to an increased risk of heart disease and stroke. A recent study showed that elevated homocysteine levels in patients were returned to normal when they were given folic acid supplements.[4]

In conclusion: A lowfat vegetarian plan is high in fiber and folic acid, moderate in protein, and low in fat. By incorporating a plan rich in vegetables, fruits, beans and enriched grains, we reduce the risk of heart disease by:

❖ Lowering saturated fat and cholesterol intake to reduce the damage the LDL-cholesterol fragment causes to arteries.

❖ Increasing our fiber intake which reduces the absorption of dietary cholesterol and lowers total blood cholesterol.

❖ Controlling the damage caused by elevated homocysteine levels.

[4] Ubblink, J.B. Vermaak, W. J. H. et al; "Vitamin B12, vitamin B6 and folate nutritional status in men with hyperhomocycsteinemia. *American Journal of Clinical Nutrition.* 1993, 57:47.

Chapter 4

Stocking the Vegetarian Kitchen

Adopting and maintaining a lowfat vegetarian dietary plan takes some preparation. Stocking your kitchen so that the ingredients you need are readily available can help you avoid choosing a food that doesn't meet your dietary goals. Following are some key ingredients that you should try to keep in your kitchen.

Beans

I encourage you to try the various types of beans available in most supermarkets. Although the recipes in this book usually call for kidney or pinto, you can substitute any similar kind of bean. Whether you use dry or canned beans is up to you. Both varieties are high in protein, iron and fiber. Unlike some other starchy vegetables, dry beans have to be cooked for a long time. In the process, they lose some vitamins but retain the protein, iron and fiber.

Hint: If you want to reduce the gassiness that beans sometimes produce, try adding a few drops of Beano® during or after cooking. This product can be found in the produce section of your supermarket, usually near the garlic or fresh spices. If you're cooking dry beans, it also helps to presoak, then drain and rinse them with water before or after cooking.

Egg Substitute

I highly recommend having nonfat egg substitute on hand as it freezes well and can be used in everything from breads and casseroles to last-minute French toast.

Soy Milk and Soy Cheese

Soy milk and soy cheese are important sources of protein and calcium for those eliminating all dairy products from their diets. You can substitute soy milk and soy cheese for milk and cheese in almost any recipe.

Tofu

Tofu is a curd made from compressed soy milk. It comes in different levels of firmness. The firmer textures appear to function better when cut into cubes. Tofu is popular in Chinese, Japanese, Thai and Indian dishes.

Tempeh

Tempeh is a cultured soy product that is very popular in Indonesia. It comes in a chunky cake form and can easily be cut into cubes for stir-frying. Tempeh has a nutty flavor and a texture that is similar to very firm tofu.

Textured Vegetable Protein (TVP®)

Also called soy protein isolate, TVP® is a concentrated form of soy protein with added flavorings. It comes in either ground, stripped or cubed forms. It is most often formed into burgers, but can be added to stir-fry or Mexican dishes. You may be able to find it in your supermarket in the form of veggie-burgers, hot dogs, sausages or even chicken nuggets. If these products are not available in your local supermarket or health food store, you may mail order from:

> The Mail Order Catalog
> P.O. Box 180
> Summertown, TN 38483
> Phone: 1-800-695-2241

Seitan

Seitan is a concentrated form of the protein found in wheat (gluten). Seitan is popular in Japan and gaining popularity in the United States. You can buy it fresh or vacuum packed (the fresh form tastes better). It can be purchased in cubed or ground forms and it has a texture similar to that of chicken. Seitan can be substituted for beef in dishes like beef stew. The ground form can be used to make burgers.

Hint: Your local health food store manager can help you order seitan.

Rice

Either brown or white rice can be used in any recipe that calls for rice. Contrary to popular belief, the nutritional content of white and brown rice are almost the same. In the United States, white rice is enriched with vitamins and minerals to match the original brown rice. There is slightly more fiber, fat and calories in the brown rice. The only real difference is flavor.

There are a few alternatives to basic white rice that are gaining popularity in the United States. *Wild rice,* grown primarily in Wisconsin, Minnesota, Louisiana and Massachusetts is a tasty alternative. *Arborio rice* is a short grain rice that Italians use almost exclusively to make their risotto recipes. *Basmati rice* is an East Indian product with a unique nutty flavor that is often toasted before cooking. And there is also a *jasmine rice* from Thailand that is good in cold dishes as it retains its fluffiness when cooled.

Be sure to follow the package directions as different kinds of rice need different cooking times. Parboiled rice (also called converted) is presoaked, steamed and dried.

I don't recommend the precooked, or instant rice. The precooking process of instant rice adversely affects the flavor and texture.

Pasta

Although my Italian heritage makes me admittedly biased, I think that pasta is one of the best foods for a vegetarian. It is popular, nutritious, easy to prepare and inexpensive. The commercial dry varieties have almost no fat, and they are fortified with vitamins and minerals (including iron, which wasn't in the original wheat). If you buy the refrigerated fresh pasta, check the label to make sure it is cholesterol-free. Stock up on several different varieties.

Breads

Because of the high volume of breads eaten by most Americans, choosing a whole-wheat bread over white bread will automatically improve your total fiber intake for the day. Oatmeal and rye breads also have more fiber than white bread. You may have difficulty getting whole-wheat breads to rise when you make them at home. If so, you can add fiber by using half wheat/half white flours, or add oatmeal or fruit to white breads.

Oatmeal and Other Cereal Products

Oatmeal is a high-fiber, lowfat grain with the most protein of all the grains. I highly recommend using oatmeal and cold cereals for snacks as well as breakfast.

Spices

I recommend developing a collection of fresh or recently purchased dried herbs and spices. Fresh flavoring makes a big difference when you're using less fat in your recipes. Remember, dried herbs should still have a strong aroma or they will need to be replaced. If you have a set of herbs and spices that you use frequently, you can combine them ahead of time in a spice blend (see instructions in *Appendix F*). You can also just match your favorite ones with the specific food (i.e., basil and oregano in tomato sauce).

Salt

Thus far I have not made dietary recommendations for salt intake; or more specifically, mentioned how much is too much. There is seldom disagreement about the need to avoid fast food restaurants, cold cuts, chips, etc., if you need to lower your salt intake. The controversy is over items like pickles, soy sauce, canned soups and fat-free cheese, which are high in salt, but low in fat. Experts generally advise people to use common sense when deciding whether or not to eat these types of foods. For example, it's important to avoid eating large portions of any salty food if you have hypertension. Of course, the rule of moderation always applies. If you're cutting high-fat, high-salt foods from your diet and losing weight, a dash of soy sauce or a few pickles won't hurt you.

Here are a few general tips for those who are concerned about their blood pressure:

❖ Consult with your doctor regarding how much of a sodium restriction you may need.

❖ Do not use the salt shaker at the table. We tend to add more salt at the table than in the cooking process.

❖ Avoid regular cheese and other salty snacks.

❖ Limit frozen entrées to the lowfat, low-sodium varieties.

❖ Avoid canned vegetables and make your own soups whenever possible.

❖ Stay clear of fast food restaurants.

Oil

Nutritionists frequently recommend olive oil or canola oil when asked what oil is best. That's because these oils are high in monounsaturated fats and low in saturated fats. Safflower, soybean, corn and sunflower oils are also acceptable oils.

Although experts love to discuss the differences among these oils, the truth is that the differences in saturated fat are not all that significant. Limiting the total amount of oil in your diet is what will make a difference to your health. In these recipes, I have recommended canola oil where I thought a lighter oil would work. For example, in baking, a light olive oil can be used for additional flavor. Otherwise, I generally use the term vegetable oil, meaning any of the oils listed above.

Supplements

Most nutritionists first advise their patients to eat a variety of healthy foods. If that is not happening, nutritionists often recommend a supplement or fortified drink. For healthy adults, the decision to take supplements is usually left to the patient.

If a person suddenly becomes a vegan vegetarian, the rules change. Americans rely on animal products as a major source of vitamin B_{12} and iron. Luckily, these nutrients can be found in enriched breads, cereals and pasta that are fortified with B_{12} and iron, as well as in nuts and beans. All other vitamins and minerals can be obtained from plant foods. One vitamin, folic acid, is known to help reduce risk of heart disease and you may want to supplement your diet to boost your protection. It is best to take folic acid in a supplement that contains all of the B vitamins.

If you decide not to eat dairy products, be sure to opt for a vitamin/mineral supplement that includes calcium. In general, I recommend a vitamin/mineral supplement to anyone drastically changing their eating habits, such as adopting a lowfat vegetarian eating plan. Unless recommended by your physician, there is no need to go over 100 percent of the RDA or to invest in expensive brand-name supplements.

The Trip to the Supermarket

Many of us have experienced searching the aisles of the supermarket unsuccessfully for something different for supper; then later deciding on a recipe for which we don't have the ingredients. Even if you're not an organized person by nature, you may want to try making out a grocery list with recipes in mind; then save it on your refrigerator to remind you of what you need.

Here's a sample grocery list. (If you have a home computer, you can save them in a file.)

Weekly Food Items	non-Food	Recipe #1
bread	dish detergent	hummus
juice	napkins	2 cans chickpeas
nonfat egg substitute	tin foil	lemon juice
fat free cheese		parsley
English muffin		garlic powder
skim milk		
tea		Recipe #2
cereal		
salad items		rice pilaf
tofu		green beans
broccoli		frozen corn
potatoes		pepper
pasta		curry
popcorn		powder
fruit		cashews

Chapter 5

Appetizers, Dips, Dressings & Sauces

Appetizers, Dips, Dressings & Sauces

Nutrisystem®

erving suggestion

DOUBLE-DOWN DEAL:

50% OFF + 50% OFF
A MONTH OF MEALS   A MONTH OF SHAKES

🚚 FREE HOME DELIVERY

†off regular one-time rate with auto-delivery

1-866-553-3438 | nutrisystem.com/ha221

Sweet Potato Puffs

You can use either fresh or canned sweet potatoes. Fully cook the fresh
potatoes in advance. Cut out and mash the pulp,
then refrigerate until cooled.

18 PUFFS

2	cups mashed sweet potatoes
1	teaspoon cinnamon
¼	teaspoon nutmeg
2	tablespoons granulated brown sugar
¼	cup nonfat egg substitute
¾	cup cornmeal
¼	cup cornmeal, for rolling
	Nonfat cooking spray
	Sweet honey mustard sauce for dipping (optional)

Combine all ingredients, except cornmeal, and form into 18—2-inch balls.
Roll in cornmeal. Place on a cookie sheet sprayed with cooking spray.

Bake for 25 to 30 minutes at 350°F.

Prep/bake time: 50 minutes

NUTRITIONAL ANALYSIS PER SERVING:
Serving Size: 3 puffs

Calories:	150	Cholesterol	0
Protein:	4 g	Fiber:	3 g
Carbohydrate:	31 g	Sodium:	340 mg
Fat:	1 g	Calcium	23 mg
		Iron	1 mg

Diabetic Exchanges: 2 starches

Stuffed Mushrooms

These are very easy and a great way to curb your appetite to avoid over-eating.

5 SERVINGS

15 large mushrooms
½ cup nonfat cottage cheese
¼ cup seasoned bread crumbs
1 teaspoon sweet green pickle relish
Dash of garlic salt (or powder)
Nonfat cooking spray

Wash mushrooms. Remove stems by twisting them. Place caps on baking sheet. Chop stems into small pieces (to make about ⅔ cup). Combine with remaining ingredients. Stuff mushrooms generously.
Spray mushrooms with cooking spray. Broil for 8 to 10 minutes.

Sprinkle with a little paprika, if desired.

Prep/bake time: 30 minutes

NUTRITIONAL ANALYSIS PER SERVING:
Serving Size: 3 mushrooms

Calories:	55	Cholesterol	0
Protein:	5 g	Fiber:	1 g
Carbohydrate:	7 g	Sodium:	260 mg
Fat:	1 g	Calcium	23 mg
		Iron	1 mg

Diabetic Exchanges: 1 protein

Bean Dip

This dip is good on crackers and adds protein to your daily intake.

6 SERVINGS

1	16-ounce container nonfat cottage cheese, pressed and drained to reduce liquid
1	Tablespoon sweet green pickle relish
½	cup kidney beans, rinsed and drained
1	Tablespoon minced onion
1	Tablespoon chives

Combine all ingredients. Serve chilled.

Prep time: 15 minutes

NUTRITIONAL ANALYSIS PER SERVING:
Serving Size: ¼ cup

Calories:	70	Cholesterol	5 mg
Protein:	11 g	Fiber:	1 g
Carbohydrate:	7 g	Sodium:	250 mg
Fat:	0	Calcium	42 mg
		Iron	1 mg

Diabetic Exchanges: 1 protein

Spicy Bean Dip

This dip works well spread on a flour tortilla and rolled up.

4 SERVINGS

1	cup of cooked pinto beans, rinsed and drained
1	clove garlic, minced (or ½ teaspoon prepared minced garlic)
1	teaspoon olive oil
2	teaspoons lemon juice
½	cup Picanté sauce (mild)
½	teaspoon cumin

Combine all ingredients in a blender and blend until smooth. Serve chilled.

Prep time: 15 minutes

NUTRITIONAL ANALYSIS PER SERVING:
Serving Size: ¼ cup

Calories:	80	Cholesterol	0
Protein:	4 g	Fiber:	1 g
Carbohydrate:	13 g	Sodium:	210 mg
Fat:	1 g	Calcium	21 mg
		Iron	1 mg

Diabetic Exchanges: 1 starch

Kidney Bean Dip

I recommend you prebake your garlic to reduce the sharpness of the flavor.
Wrap garlic cloves in tin foil and bake in the oven at 400°F for about 10 minutes.

8 SERVINGS

½   cup reduced calorie Miracle Whip® dressing
     (or nonfat creamy dressing)
2   Tablespoons sweet green pickle relish
1   clove garlic
1   15-ounce can kidney beans, rinsed
     and drained

Combine the dressing, relish, and garlic in a bowl; add kidney beans. Place half of the mixture in a blender and pulse blend until most or all of the beans are puréed. Remove and place in a covered storage container. Repeat with the second half of the mixture. There may be some whole beans left and the dip will have a thick paste consistency.

Refrigerate and serve cold with crackers.

Prep time: 20 minutes

NUTRITIONAL ANALYSIS PER SERVING:
Serving Size: ¼ cup

Calories:	110	Cholesterol	0
Protein:	5 g	Fiber:	4 g
Carbohydrate:	17 g	Sodium:	130 mg
Fat:	3 g	Calcium	18 mg
		Iron	2 mg

Diabetic Exchanges: 1 starch

Bread 'n Butter Pickles

*This sounds like a lot of sugar and salt, but most of it remains
soluble in the brine.*

20 SERVINGS

5   fresh pickling cucumbers
2   cups cider vinegar
1   cup sugar
2   Tablespoons pickling spice
1   Tablespoon salt
2   cups water

Wash and slice cucumbers. Place cucumbers in 2-quart container with a
cover (you can use a plastic storage container).

Add vinegar, sugar, spice, and salt to a saucepan. Heat to boiling, stirring
frequently. Let stand for 5 minutes off the heat. Pour over the cucumbers
and cover with water, adding more water if necessary to cover.

Refrigerate. Can be kept up to six weeks refrigerated.

If you want to remove the pickling spice the next day, you can remove the
pickles and place in a separate container. Pour the liquid through a strainer
into the new container with the pickles. Refrigerate.

Prep/cook time: 20 minutes, not including refrigeration

NUTRITIONAL ANALYSIS PER SERVING:
Serving Size: 4 pickles

Calories:	20	Cholesterol	0
Protein:	1 g	Fiber:	0
Carbohydrate:	4 g	Sodium:	170 mg
Fat:	0	Calcium	14 mg
		Iron	0

Diabetic Exchanges: 1 vegetable

Corn Relish

*This makes a good side dish for a Mexican or Indian meal, such as chili or a
curry dish. It can be stored up to 2 weeks in the refrigerator.*

3 SERVINGS

¼ cup cider vinegar
3 Tablespoons sugar
¼ teaspoon salt
¼ teaspoon dry mustard
Dash of cumin
1 cup cooked corn* (2 leftover ears)
¼ cup diced onion
¼ cup diced sweet pepper

Combine vinegar, sugar, salt, and spices in a saucepan and bring to a boil.
Add vegetables and cook for 4 to 5 minutes. Cool and place in a clean
glass jar. Refrigerate.

* I used leftover fresh corn cut from the cob, but frozen will work also.

Prep/cook time: 20 minutes

NUTRITIONAL ANALYSIS PER SERVING:
Serving Size: ⅓ cup

Calories:	100	Cholesterol	0
Protein:	2 g	Fiber:	2 g
Carbohydrate:	24 g	Sodium:	180 mg
Fat:	0	Calcium	5 mg
		Iron	0

Diabetic Exchanges: 1 starch

Nutty Wontons

Serve as an appetizer or a side dish. You can save prep time
by purchasing a package of cole slaw vegetables, already shredded.

12 WONTONS

	Package of 24 wonton wrappers
2	cloves garlic, crushed
1	Tablespoon olive oil
¼	cup vegetable broth
1	Tablespoon light soy sauce
½	cabbage, shredded
1	large (or 2 small) carrots, shredded
2	cups fresh bean sprouts
1	teaspoon ginger
1	teaspoon hot sesame oil (optional)
½	cup dry roasted peanuts, crushed in blender or processor
¼	cup nonfat egg substitute (plus a little for coating)
	Nonfat cooking spray

Preheat oven to 375°F. Sauté the garlic in olive oil for a minute. Add the broth, soy sauce, vegetables, spices, and sesame oil. Simmer until vegetables are wilted and almost fully cooked. Meanwhile, lightly coat a 12 cup muffin tin with cooking spray. Place 12 wonton wrappers in the muffin tin, one in each cup. Remove sauté pan from heat. When cooled to lukewarm temperature, add peanuts and egg substitute. Fill the wonton wrappers in the muffin tin with vegetable filling and place another wonton wrapper on top of each of the 12 wontons. Fold corners in and seal by brushing a thin coat of egg substitute over them with a pastry brush. Bake at 375°F for 10 to 12 minutes, or until edges start to look dark brown and crispy. **Prep/cook time: 50 minutes**

NUTRITIONAL ANALYSIS PER SERVING:
Serving Size: 1 wonton

Calories:	110	Cholesterol	0
Protein:	5 g	Fiber:	2 g
Carbohydrate:	14 g	Sodium:	140 mg
Fat:	4 g	Calcium	36 mg
		Iron	1 mg

Diabetic Exchanges: 1 starch, 1 vegetable

Salsa

*This is a simple fresh salsa for those who are afraid of hot chili pepper seeds.
Chili pepper can be added if you wish. Diced sweet pepper
or parsley could also be added.*

4 SERVINGS

3	medium tomatoes, diced small
½	cup finely chopped onion
1	Tablespoon lime juice
1	Tablespoon fresh cilantro, chopped (or ½ Tablespoon dried)
1	large or 2 small cloves garlic*
⅛	teaspoon cayenne pepper
½	teaspoon salt

Combine all ingredients and chill before serving. Serve with rice or corn tortillas, baked in the oven until crispy.

To make tortilla chips: Place 2 or 3 corn tortillas on a cookie sheet and spray with cooking spray. Bake 400°F for 8 to 10 minutes, or until crispy. Cut tortillas into 6 triangles.

*Prepare garlic as follows: Wrap in foil and place in oven for about 10 minutes at 400°F. Finely dice the garlic and add to salsa.

Prep time: 25 minutes

NUTRITIONAL ANALYSIS PER SERVING:
Serving Size: ½ cup

Calories:	30	Cholesterol	0
Protein:	1 g	Fiber:	1 g
Carbohydrate:	6 g	Sodium:	140 mg
Fat:	0	Calcium	8 mg
		Iron	1 mg

Diabetic Exchanges: 1 vegetable

Barbecue Sauce

This sauce is terrific over prepared soyburgers or veggie-burgers.

6 SERVINGS

2	cups tomato juice
1	Tablespoon canola oil
½	teaspoon pepper
⅛	teaspoon cayenne pepper
1	Tablespoon Worcestershire sauce
¼	cup vinegar
½	teaspoon prepared or fresh minced garlic
1	bay leaf (optional)
1	teaspoon cornstarch (optional)

Combine all ingredients in a saucepan. Simmer about 20 minutes, or until mixture thickens to a sauce consistency. You can sprinkle, then blend in, about a teaspoon of cornstarch to thicken faster. Remove bay leaf.

Prep/cook time: 35 minutes

NUTRITIONAL ANALYSIS PER SERVING:
Serving Size: ¼ cup

Calories:	35	Cholesterol	0
Protein:	1 g	Fiber:	0
Carbohydrate:	4 g	Sodium:	290 mg
Fat:	2 g	Calcium	15 mg
		Iron	1 mg

Diabetic Exchanges: 1 vegetable

Mushroom Gravy

This is a basic gravy recipe that can be used for the Millet Patties on page 160, Vegetarian Meatloaf on page 157, Peanutty Carrot Loaf on page 121, or Soy-Oat Burgers on page 122.

8 SERVINGS

1 medium onion, chopped
1 cup chopped fresh mushrooms
1 Tablespoon safflower or canola oil
2 Tablespoons white wine (optional)
1 Tablespoon cornstarch
1 cup water
¼ cup light soy sauce
Parsley

In a skillet, sauté the onion and mushrooms in the oil for a minute. Add wine for moisture, if desired. Add the soy sauce to the cornstarch mixture and pour over the vegetables. Cook until thickened to gravy consistency. While it is cooking, chop a little parsley as garnish, if so desired.

Prep/cook time: 20 minutes

NUTRITIONAL ANALYSIS PER SERVING:
Serving Size: ¼ cup

Calories:	35	Cholesterol	0
Protein:	1 g	Fiber:	0
Carbohydrate:	4 g	Sodium:	250 mg
Fat:	2 g	Calcium	5 mg
		Iron	0

Diabetic Exchanges: 1 vegetable

Marinara Sauce

If you've got an herb garden, this is a nice way to use those fresh herbs. Boil the water for the pasta while the sauce is simmering.

6 SERVINGS

2   teaspoons olive oil
1   medium onion, chopped
12   fresh tomatoes, chopped
4   cloves garlic, minced with garlic press
1   Tablespoon fresh basil (or 2 teaspoons dried)
¼   teaspoon fresh or dried oregano
½   teaspoon salt
1   bay leaf

Combine all ingredients in a saucepan and cook on medium heat for 15 to 20 minutes. Press through a sieve or strainer and store in a quart-size container in the refrigerator. Serve hot with pasta.

Prep/cook time: 30 minutes

NUTRITIONAL ANALYSIS PER SERVING:
Serving Size: ½ cup

Calories:	70	Cholesterol	0
Protein:	2 g	Fiber:	2 g
Carbohydrate:	13 g	Sodium:	200 mg
Fat:	1 g	Calcium	16 mg
		Iron	1 mg

Diabetic Exchanges: 2 vegetables

Lentil Tomato Sauce

This sauce is good over stuffed peppers. If you use fresh tomatoes, add ½ teaspoon of salt. Do not add salt if using canned tomatoes.

6 SERVINGS

2½ cups chopped tomatoes
½ cup red lentils, dry
½ cup water
1 small onion, chopped
2 cloves garlic, minced
1 teaspoon basil
1 teaspoon oregano
1 Tablespoon fresh parsley
½ teaspoon salt, as needed
Dash cayenne pepper

Place all ingredients in a saucepan and simmer until lentils are tender, approximately 20 minutes. Place ingredients in a blender and process until smooth. Return to saucepan and heat before serving, adding more water, if necessary, to desired consistency.

Serve hot over stuffed peppers or store in a tight-lid container for up to two weeks in the refrigerator.

Prep/cook time: 35 minutes

NUTRITIONAL ANALYSIS PER SERVING:			
Serving Size: ½ cup			
Calories:	80	Cholesterol	0
Protein:	5 g	Fiber:	3 g
Carbohydrate:	14 g	Sodium:	170 mg
Fat:	0	Calcium	16 mg
		Iron	2 mg

Diabetic Exchanges: 1 starch

Pasta Sauce with Sun-Dried Tomatoes

This makes a thick, chunky sauce with the fresh tomatoes; you can add a little water and purée them if you wish. I don't feel that you need to seed the tomatoes first. But if you prefer seedless, purchase a can of seeded tomatoes.

6 SERVINGS

1	small onion, chopped
2-3	cloves garlic, minced
1	teaspoon olive oil
4	cups chopped ripe tomatoes (or 1—28-ounce can chopped tomatoes)
½	cup (about 12 pieces) reconstituted sun-dried tomatoes, finely chopped
1	teaspoon dried basil or 2 teaspoons fresh basil
2	Tablespoons parsley
½	teaspoon oregano
½	teaspoon salt

In a saucepan, sauté onion and garlic in the oil for a minute. Add remaining ingredients and heat for 20 minutes. Serve hot over pasta.

Prep/cook time: 35 minutes

NUTRITIONAL ANALYSIS PER SERVING:
Serving Size: ½ cup

Calories:	45	Cholesterol	0
Protein:	2 g	Fiber:	2 g
Carbohydrate:	7 g	Sodium:	280 mg
Fat:	1 g	Calcium	20 mg
		Iron	1 mg

Diabetic Exchanges: 1 vegetable

Basic White Sauce for Pasta

This creamy white sauce thickens up quickly, so you will want to put the water on for the pasta before you start the sauce.

4 SERVINGS

1   small onion, chopped
½   cup white wine
2   Tablespoons light cream cheese,
       preferably garlic or herb-flavored
1½ Tablespoons flour
1¼ cups 1% lowfat milk
¼   teaspoon salt
       Dash of pepper

Gather the ingredients on your counter so that you may add them quickly. In a saucepan, simmer the onion in the wine for a minute. Add the cream cheese while stirring. Then sprinkle the flour over the mixture, still stirring, as the cheese melts. Add milk and seasoning; then continue stirring over medium heat until the sauce thickens to the desired consistency.

Prep/cook time: 20 minutes

NUTRITIONAL ANALYSIS PER SERVING:
Serving Size: ½ cup

Calories:	65	Cholesterol	5 mg
Protein:	3 g	Fiber:	1 g
Carbohydrate:	8 g	Sodium:	190 mg
Fat:	2 g	Calcium	81 mg
		Iron	0

Diabetic Exchanges: 1 milk

Pumpkin & Cheese Sauce for Pasta

This alternative to tomato sauce cooks fast. You may want to start the water for the pasta first; either dry fettuccine, ziti, or even bow tie will go well with this. The pumpkin makes it rich in beta-carotene.

4 SERVINGS

2   cups vegetable broth*
1   teaspoon cornstarch
½   cup 1% cottage cheese
1   15-ounce can mashed pumpkin
1   large clove garlic
¼   teaspoon ground ginger
     Dash of pepper
     A few fresh scallions for garnish, if desired

Combine the cornstarch with a little broth to blend in; then add all ingredients except the scallions to a blender. Purée until smooth. Then add to either a double boiler or saucepan on low heat. Cook for only about 10 minutes; do not let the sauce boil. Pour immediately over hot, drained pasta. Sprinkle with scallions, if desired.

*If you're using a low sodium broth, add ½ teaspoon salt to the mixture. Homemade broth is preferred over commercial broths.

Prep/cook time: 40 minutes

NUTRITIONAL ANALYSIS PER SERVING, WITHOUT PASTA:
Serving Size: ½ cup

Calories:	70	Cholesterol	0
Protein:	5 g	Fiber:	3 g
Carbohydrate:	11 g	Sodium:	260 mg
Fat:	1 g	Calcium	48 mg
		Iron	2 mg

Diabetic Exchanges: 1 starch

Cannellini Carrot Sauce for Pasta

The beans and milk in this sauce complement the protein in the pasta.
You can make the sauce thinner or thicker by slowly adding the milk, adding
more if necessary to get the desired consistency.

8 SERVINGS

6	cloves garlic, whole
1	small onion, chopped
1	teaspoon olive oil
½	cup white wine
3	cups water
3	raw carrots, sliced (or 1 cup frozen)
7-8	pieces sun-dried tomatoes, reconstituted and chopped
1	cup of cooked cannellini beans, rinsed and drained
1	teaspoon fresh basil (or ½ teaspoon dried)
¼	teaspoon oregano
1	teaspoon salt
1	bay leaf
1	cup skim milk

In a saucepan, sauté garlic and onion in the oil for a minute. Add the wine and cook for another few minutes. Add remaining ingredients, except for the milk. Heat for 15 to 20 minutes, until the carrots are done. Remove bay leaf and add ingredients to a blender. Purée for 8 to 10 seconds. Return to saucepan, add milk, and heat thoroughly.

Prep/cook time: 45 minutes

NUTRITIONAL ANALYSIS PER SERVING:
Serving Size: ⅔ cup

Calories:	65	Cholesterol	0
Protein:	3 g	Fiber:	3 g
Carbohydrate:	12 g	Sodium:	430 mg
Fat:	1 g	Calcium	62 mg
		Iron	1 mg

Diabetic Exchanges: 2 vegetables

Sweet Pepper Pasta Sauce

*This is a simple fresh sauce; best started
after you put the water on to boil for the pasta.*

5 SERVINGS

3-4 cloves garlic, crushed
1   teaspoon olive oil
3   large or 4 small fresh tomatoes,
    cut in small pieces
2   sweet red peppers, cut in small pieces
½   cup white wine
½   teaspoon salt
1   Tablespoon fresh basil
    (or ½ Tablespoon dried)

After you have cut the vegetables, sauté the garlic in the oil for a minute.
Add remaining ingredients and simmer until you have the desired
consistency for pasta sauce—about 15 minutes. Serve over pasta.

Prep/cook time: 30 minutes

NUTRITIONAL ANALYSIS PER SERVING:
Serving Size: ½ cup

Calories:	40	Cholesterol	0
Protein:	1 g	Fiber:	2 g
Carbohydrate:	7 g	Sodium:	220 mg
Fat:	1 g	Calcium	8 mg
		Iron	1 mg

Diabetic Exchanges: 1 vegetable

Ginger Sauce for Burritos

You can substitute this simple sauce for the black bean sauce in the Veggie-Burritos with Black Bean Sauce recipe on page 120. You can also use it for any other Oriental stir-fry dish. It stores well for weeks in the refrigerator.

6 SERVINGS

1½   cups water
½   cup light soy sauce
1   2-inch piece ginger, grated
     (or 1 teaspoon ground ginger)
2   Tablespoons cornstarch
¼   cup water

Combine first 3 ingredients in a sauce pan and bring to a boil. Reduce heat, combine cornstarch and ¼ cup water and add to saucepan. Simmer until thickened.

Prep/cook time: 20 minutes

NUTRITIONAL ANALYSIS PER SERVING: *Serving Size: ¼ cup*			
Calories:	20	Cholesterol	0
Protein:	1 g	Fiber:	0
Carbohydrate:	4 g	Sodium:	670 mg
Fat:	0	Calcium	0
		Iron	0

Diabetic Exchanges: Free

Creamy Mustard Vinaigrette

This is great on a pasta salad or a tossed green salad.

14 SERVINGS

¾   cup water
¼   cup olive oil
½   cup apple cider vinegar (or balsamic)
1   Tablespoon prepared mustard (any type)
2   Tablespoons light mayo-type salad dressing
1   Tablespoon lemon juice
1   Tablespoon sugar
2   teaspoons fresh basil (or 1 teaspoon dried)
1   teaspoon dried parsley
1   teaspoon salt
    Dash of pepper

Combine all ingredients in a covered container. Shake well before serving.

Prep time: 15 minutes

NUTRITIONAL ANALYSIS PER SERVING: *Serving Size: 2 Tablespoons*			
Calories:	40	Cholesterol	0
Protein:	0	Fiber:	0
Carbohydrate:	2 g	Sodium:	170 mg
Fat:	4 g	Calcium	3 mg
		Iron	0

Diabetic Exchanges: 1 fat

Sweet Raspberry Vinaigrette

*This is a popular light dressing that is actually quite easy to make.
You can make 8 ounces, as shown; or double the portions
if you intend to use it frequently.*

8 SERVINGS

1	clove garlic, crushed
1	teaspoon olive oil
½	cup raspberry vinegar (see below)
½	cup water
1	teaspoon cornstarch
¼	teaspoon salt

In a small saucepan, sauté garlic in oil for a minute. Add remaining
ingredients and cook until it thickens a little.

Cool and store in a tight-lid jar.

Raspberry Vinegar

½	cup fresh or frozen raspberries
1	cup cider vinegar
½	cup sugar

Purée berries and vinegar in a blender and add this, with the sugar, to a
saucepan. Simmer 10 minutes. Cool and store in an empty vinegar jar or
other tight-lid jar.

Prep/cook time: 40 minutes

NUTRITIONAL ANALYSIS PER SERVING:
Serving Size: 2 Tablespoons

Calories:	35	Cholesterol	0
Protein:	0	Fiber:	0
Carbohydrate:	7 g	Sodium:	65 mg
Fat:	1 g	Calcium	2 mg
		Iron	0

Diabetic Exchanges: 1 fruit

Chapter 6

Soups & Salads

Soups

Salads

Homemade Vegetable Broth

With this recipe you can remove some of the broth to store and make soup for the evening.

4 CUPS OF BROTH OR 6 CUPS OF SOUP

1	onion, chopped in large chunks
2	large carrots, peeled and sliced
2	celery stalks, sliced
2	potatoes, washed well, then peeled and chopped
2	Tablespoons dried parsley
1	teaspoon dried oregano (or basil)
1	bay leaf
1	teaspoon salt
	Dash of pepper
2	quarts water

In a large soup pot, combine all ingredients. Bring to a boil, then lower heat and simmer 30 minutes. With a measuring cup, remove 4 cups of broth and pour through a strainer into a large storage container. Refrigerate broth. To remaining stock in pot, add about 2 cups water if you wish to make soup. Heat another 10 minutes and serve.

Prep/cook time: 1 hour

NUTRITIONAL ANALYSIS PER SERVING:
Serving Size: 1 cup of soup (Broth contains essentially no calories.)

Calories:	90	Cholesterol	0
Protein:	3 g	Fiber:	5 g
Carbohydrate:	18 g	Sodium:	200 mg
Fat:	trace	Calcium	52 mg
		Iron	0

Diabetic Exchanges: 1 starch, 1 vegetable

Tomato Orzo Soup

Serve with oyster crackers and fruit to complete a winter lunch. This is better with the homemade broth, but you need to start the broth an hour before you plan to eat.

6 SERVINGS

1	teaspoon olive oil
1	clove garlic, crushed
1	20-ounce can tomato purée
3	cups vegetable broth*
1	bay leaf
¼	teaspoon thyme (or oregano)
	Dash of pepper
½	cup dry orzo pasta (about 1½ cups cooked)
1½	cups skim milk

Sauté garlic in the oil in a soup pot for only 30 seconds. Add the tomato purée, broth, herbs, and pepper. Simmer about 15 minutes. Meanwhile, cook pasta in a separate saucepan. Drain pasta and add it, with the milk, to the soup pot. Heat, but do not boil.

*Use either prepared salt-free vegetable broth or make your own, see page 65.

Prep/cook time: 1 hour, with homemade broth

NUTRITIONAL ANALYSIS PER SERVING:
Serving Size: 1½ cups

Calories:	120	Cholesterol:	0
Protein:	6 g	Fiber:	3 g
Carbohydrate:	24 g	Sodium:	410 mg
Fat:	1 g	Calcium	92 mg
		Iron	2 mg

Diabetic Exchanges: 1 starch, 2 vegetables

Herbed Italian Stew

This stew makes a hearty lunch served with a salad, a slice of Italian bread, and perhaps a glass of red wine. A combination of fresh Italian herbs (see Appendix F on page 248) instead of dried herbs works well with this recipe.

4 SERVINGS

1	Tablespoon olive oil
1	onion, chopped
1	clove garlic, minced
2	14-ounce cans vegetable broth
2½	cups water
2	fresh tomatoes, chopped
1	cup chopped zucchini or Italian green beans
½	teaspoon dried basil
½	teaspoon dried rosemary
½	cup dry orzo or any tiny pasta
½	cup lowfat shredded Cheddar cheese (optional)

In a stew pot, sauté the onion and garlic in oil. Add remaining ingredients, except the cheese and pasta. Cook about 20 minutes, then add the pasta. Cook another 12 minutes. Spoon into bowls and top with cheese, if desired.

Prep/cook time: 45 minutes

NUTRITIONAL ANALYSIS PER SERVING WITHOUT CHEESE:
Serving Size: 1½ cups

Calories:	140	Cholesterol	0
Protein:	4 g	Fiber:	2 g
Carbohydrate:	24 g	Sodium:	290 mg
Fat:	3 g	Calcium	21 mg
		Iron	1 mg

Diabetic Exchanges: 1 starch, 2 vegetables

Pasta Fagioli, I

This version has a thicker stew-like consistency than most soups.
Just add more water if you like it thinner. Use fresh herbs in this recipe,
if available; it makes a difference.

8 SERVINGS

8	ounces (3 cups) elbow or small shells macaroni, uncooked
2	teaspoons olive oil
1	onion, diced
½	fresh green pepper, chopped
1	large or 2 small cloves garlic, crushed
2	cups vegetable broth
4	cups water
1	Tablespoon fresh parsley
1	teaspoon fresh or dried basil
2	fresh tomatoes, chopped
1	28-ounce can crushed tomatoes, salt-free
1	cup cooked beans, rinsed well (pinto or cannellini)
	Dash of cayenne pepper or black pepper

In a saucepan cook and drain the pasta. In a large skillet, sauté the onion, pepper, and garlic in the oil for a few minutes. Add remaining ingredients and cook for about 15 minutes. Combine the sauce with the pasta. Serve with fresh bread.

Prep/cook time: 35 minutes

NUTRITIONAL ANALYSIS PER SERVING:
Serving Size: 1¾ cups

Calories:	210	Cholesterol:	0
Protein:	10 g	Fiber:	6 g
Carbohydrate:	39 g	Sodium:	520 mg
Fat:	2 g	Calcium	60 mg
		Iron	4 mg

Diabetic Exchanges: 2 starches, 2 vegetables

Pasta Fagioli, II

This is a tomato-free version of an Italian classic.

6 SERVINGS

2	cups small shells or elbow pasta, uncooked
½	medium onion, chopped
1	Tablespoon olive oil
6	cups water or low-sodium vegetable broth
3	carrots, peeled and sliced
3	cloves garlic, minced
1	8-ounce package frozen Italian green beans
1	15-ounce can white or cannellini beans
1	teaspoon oregano
1	Tablespoon parsley
1	teaspoon salt
	Pepper to taste

Add oil to a large saucepan. Sauté onion until just tender. Add broth and carrots. In a separate saucepan, bring 2 quarts of water to a boil and cook the pasta. Meanwhile add remaining ingredients to the carrot and onion mixture. When the pasta is cooked, drain and add to the saucepan. Cook until carrots are tender.

Prep/cook time: 35 minutes

NUTRITIONAL ANALYSIS PER SERVING:
Serving Size: 1¾ cups

Calories:	260	Cholesterol	0
Protein:	11 g	Fiber:	8 g
Carbohydrate:	48 g	Sodium:	290 mg
Fat:	3 g	Calcium	73 mg
		Iron	4 mg

Diabetic Exchanges: 2 starches, 1 protein, 1 vegetable

Split Pea Soup with Italian Herbs

This soup is easy to assemble and is ready to eat in 60 minutes. You can use either fresh or dried herbs. Remember, dried herbs should still have a strong aroma or they will need to be replaced.

4 SERVINGS

7	cups water
2	cups dry green split peas
1	carrot, chopped
1	small onion, diced
1	large or 2 small cloves garlic (pressed through garlic press)
1	teaspoon fresh basil (or ½ teaspoon dried)
½	teaspoon fresh oregano (or ¼ teaspoon dried)
1	teaspoon parsley
1	teaspoon salt
1	bay leaf

Combine water and split peas in a saucepan. Cook on medium heat for 20 minutes. Add remaining ingredients, then reduce heat and simmer for 30 minutes more. Serve with Italian bread.

Prep/cook time: 1 hour

NUTRITIONAL ANALYSIS PER SERVING:
Serving Size: 1½ cups

Calories:	190	Cholesterol:	0
Protein:	13 g	Fiber:	5 g
Carbohydrate:	34 g	Sodium:	290 mg
Fat:	1 g	Calcium	40 mg
		Iron	2 mg

Diabetic Exchanges: 2 starches, 1 protein

Pumpkin Soup

Try this for a nourishing and filling cool-weather appetizer.

3 SERVINGS

1	Tablespoon vegetable oil
1	small onion, chopped
2	cups vegetable stock or broth
1	15-ounce can pumpkin
½	teaspoon nutmeg
1	bay leaf
½	teaspoon salt
	Pepper to taste
1	cup evaporated skim milk
	Chives for garnish, if desired

In a large soup pot, sauté onion in the oil. Add the remaining ingredients, except the milk. Cook about 10 to 15 minutes over medium heat. Add milk and heat thoroughly, but do not boil. Remove bay leaf and garnish with chives.

Prep/cook time: 25 minutes

NUTRITIONAL ANALYSIS PER SERVING:
Serving Size: 1¾ cups

Calories:	130	Cholesterol	0
Protein:	5 g	Fiber:	5 g
Carbohydrate:	18 g	Sodium:	410 mg
Fat:	4 g	Calcium	132 mg
		Iron	1 mg

Diabetic Exchanges: 1 starch, 1 vegetable

Andrea's Pumpkin Soup

This makes a warm and satisfying winter lunch. You can use fresh or canned pumpkin.

6 SERVINGS

8	cups of water
6	cups cooked, mashed pumpkin
2	stalks celery, sliced
3	carrots, sliced
1	onion, chopped
1	Tablespoon curry powder
½	teaspoon ginger
1	teaspoon allspice
½	teaspoon dill (optional)
1	teaspoon salt and pepper to taste

In a large soup pot, combine all ingredients and cook until soft; about 20 minutes. Purée in a blender until smooth. Return to heat and adjust seasonings to taste.

Prep/cook time: 40 minutes

NUTRITIONAL ANALYSIS PER SERVING:
Serving Size: 2 cups

Calories:	110	Cholesterol:	0
Protein:	3 g	Fiber:	8 g
Carbohydrate:	25 g	Sodium:	390 mg
Fat:	trace	Calcium:	83 mg
		Iron	4 mg

Diabetic Exchanges: 1 starch, 1 vegetable

Orange-Butternut Soup

You can use either fresh or frozen squash, but fresh will give you better flavor.

4 SERVINGS

Vegetable broth:

2   quarts water
1   large butternut squash, skinned and cut in chunks
1   bunch (4-5) scallions, chopped
2   carrots, peeled and cut in chunks
¾   teaspoon salt

Soup:

1   Spanish onion, chopped
1   Tablespoon olive oil
1   Tablespoon orange juice
¼   teaspoon nutmeg
1   bay leaf
¼   cup wine or water
½   teaspoon fresh dill or thyme
5   cups fresh vegetable broth, see above

Prepare broth ingredients in a large sauce pan and boil for about 15 minutes. Meanwhile, in a soup pot, sauté the onion in oil. Add remaining ingredients, except the broth. Simmer the onion mixture as you pour the broth mixture through a strainer into a large bowl.

Measure 2 cups of broth and pour into a blender. Add some of the squash chunks to the blender and purée. Add to the onion mixture. Repeat this with 3 more cups of broth and remaining squash. Heat another 10 minutes and remove bay leaf.

Pre/cook time: 45 minutes

NUTRITIONAL ANALYSIS PER SERVING:
Serving Size: 1½ cups

Calories:	130	Cholesterol	0
Protein:	2 g	Fiber:	6 g
Carbohydrate:	24 g	Sodium:	420 mg
Fat:	3 g	Calcium	81 mg
		Iron	1 mg

Diabetic Exchanges: 1 starch, 1 vegetable

Spicy Corn Chowder

Chowder does not have to be fattening to taste rich. You can use frozen diced potatoes or leave the skin on new red potatoes if you want to save time.

4 SERVINGS

4	medium potatoes, peeled and cubed
1	Tablespoon canola or olive oil
½	large green or red pepper, chopped
½	cup chopped onion
1	cup vegetable broth
1	8-ounce package frozen corn
¼	teaspoon ground cumin
⅛	teaspoon black pepper
1½	cups skim milk
2	Tablespoons flour
1	12-ounce can of evaporated skim milk
2-3	drops hot pepper sauce (optional)

Microwave the potatoes 3 or 4 minutes, until they cut easily, but are not fully cooked.

In a large soup pot, sauté green pepper and onion in oil until tender. Add broth, corn, potatoes, cumin and pepper. Cook ten minutes more. Meanwhile, pour 1½ cups milk into bowl; whisk in flour until well-blended. Add evaporated milk and mix well. Slowly pour into saucepan. Cook on low heat for 7 to 10 minutes, stirring constantly until mixture thickens slightly. Add hot pepper sauce, if desired.

Prep/cook time: 35 minutes

NUTRITIONAL ANALYSIS PER SERVING:
Serving Size: 1½ cups

Calories:	280	Cholesterol:	0
Protein:	18 g	Fiber:	2 g
Carbohydrate:	46 g	Sodium:	230 mg
Fat:	4 g	Calcium	563 mg
		Iron	1 mg

Diabetic Exchanges: 2 starches, 1 milk, 1 vegetable

Corn Tortilla Soup

*I recommend using fresh limes here—it's a key ingredient in this soup.
The type of tomato or pepper you use is optional and you can vary the amount of
spice. You may want to use a vegetable broth; but remember to dilute the cans
with water as they tend to be salty.*

4 SERVINGS

1	small onion, chopped
1	teaspoon vegetable oil
6	cups water
2	nonfat vegetable stock cubes
1	14-ounce bag of frozen corn
1	tomato, chopped
1	sweet red pepper, chopped
½	teaspoon cumin
1	bay leaf
⅛	teaspoon cayenne pepper
2	Tablespoons fresh lime juice
½	cup cooked black beans (optional)
4	corn tortillas, made into chips

In a large soup pot, sauté the onion in oil. Add the remaining ingredients
and simmer about 30 minutes. Remove the bay leaf. Serve hot with tortilla
chips on top or on the side.

To make tortilla chips: While the soup is simmering, cut 4 corn tortillas in
half, then in strips, then in half again. Place on a cookie sheet and spray
with cooking spray; salt lightly.

Bake 10 minutes in a preheated 350°F oven.

Prep/cook time: 50 minutes

NUTRITIONAL ANALYSIS PER SERVING WITH TORTILLA:
Serving Size: 2 cups

Calories:	190	Cholesterol	0
Protein:	7 g	Fiber:	5 g
Carbohydrate:	40 g	Sodium:	570 mg
Fat:	2 g	Calcium	61 mg
		Iron	1 mg

Diabetic Exchanges: 2 starches, 1 vegetable

Corn Dumpling Soup

The key to these dumplings is to keep them small so they will be easier to eat.

8 SERVINGS

Dumplings:
1   cup yellow cornmeal
1   cup flour
2   teaspoons baking powder
2   teaspoons basil
2   scallions, chopped
½   teaspoon salt
¼   teaspoon pepper
1   Tablespoon molasses
¼   cup water
1   Tablespoon olive oil
¼   cup nonfat egg substitute

Broth:
4   scallions, chopped
1   Tablespoon olive oil
1   fresh tomato
1   16-ounce can of stewed tomatoes, blenderized
2   quarts water
1   nonfat vegetable stock cube

To make dumplings: Combine dry ingredients. Then add wet ingredients and stir to blend evenly. With moistened hands, make 32 small balls. Drop in the broth, as directed below.

To make the broth: In a skillet, sauté scallions in the oil. Add remaining ingredients and simmer for 10 minutes. Add dumplings to broth and cook for another 12 to 15 minutes. **Prep/cook time: 1 hour**

NUTRITIONAL ANALYSIS PER SERVING:
Serving Size: 1½ cups

Calories:	170	Cholesterol:	0
Protein:	6 g	Fiber:	2 g
Carbohydrate:	29 g	Sodium:	400 mg
Fat:	4 g	Calcium	59 mg
		Iron	2 mg

Diabetic Exchanges: 2 starches

Peg's Potato and Leek Soup

Leeks are a delicious alternative to onions and are available in any grocery store. The ginger complements the flavor of the potato.

6 SERVINGS

3	cups thinly sliced leeks
6	cups water
2	vegetable stock cubes
4	cups peeled and chopped potatoes (about 5 medium)
1	teaspoon ground ginger
½	teaspoon thyme
	Dash of freshly ground pepper
1	cup skim milk
	Nonfat cooking spray

Clean the leeks thoroughly before slicing. Spray the bottom of a soup pot with cooking spray. Add the leeks and sauté for a minute. Add all ingredients except milk and simmer until potatoes are cooked. Put all solid ingredients with some liquid in a blender or food processor. Return to the pot, add the skim milk and heat until the soup is hot.

Prep/cook time: 1 hour

NUTRITIONAL ANALYSIS PER SERVING:
Serving Size: 2 cups

Calories:	160	Cholesterol	0
Protein:	5 g	Fiber:	4 g
Carbohydrate:	34 g	Sodium:	400 mg
Fat:	1 g	Calcium	76 mg
		Iron	1 mg

Diabetic Exchanges: 2 starches

Tortellini Soup

This makes a warm and satisfying cold weather lunch. You can substitute frozen green beans and vary the garlic and herbs to your liking.

4 SERVINGS

1   teaspoon olive oil
5-6 cloves garlic, minced
8   cups water
1   nonfat vegetable stock cube
1   small or ½ large sweet red pepper, chopped
1   cup cut fresh green beans
1   8-ounce package fresh cheese tortellini
1   teaspoon dried or fresh basil
¼   teaspoon black pepper

In a soup pot, sauté the garlic in the oil. Add the water with bouillon and bring to a boil. Add the remaining ingredients. Cook on medium heat approximately 15 minutes or until pasta is done.

Prep/cook time: 30 minutes

NUTRITIONAL ANALYSIS PER SERVING:
Serving Size: 1½ cups

Calories:	230	Cholesterol:	30 mg
Protein:	12 g	Fiber:	1 g
Carbohydrate:	32 g	Sodium:	510 mg
Fat:	7 g	Calcium:	15 mg
		Iron	0

Diabetic Exchanges: 1 starch, 1 protein, 1 fat, 1 vegetable

Lentil Noodle Soup

This fresh alternative to canned chicken noodle is a cinch to prepare.

6 SERVINGS

1	teaspoon olive oil
1	onion, diced
2	cloves garlic, minced
1	cup dry lentils
2	quarts water
2	carrots, sliced
2	nonfat vegetable stock cubes
⅔	cup dry noodles (elbows, corkscrews)
1	cup chopped kale or watercress

In a skillet, sauté onion and garlic in the oil for 2 minutes. Add lentils, water, carrots, and bouillon and cook approximately 40 to 50 minutes. Add noodles and boil another 10 minutes. Add kale and cook a few minutes more.

Garnish with fresh parsley, if desired.

Prep/cook time: 1¼ hours

NUTRITIONAL ANALYSIS PER SERVING:
Serving Size: 1½ cups

Calories:	210	Cholesterol	0
Protein:	12 g	Fiber:	6 g
Carbohydrate:	39 g	Sodium:	200 mg
Fat:	1 g	Calcium	41 mg
		Iron	4 mg

Diabetic Exchanges: 2 starches, 1 protein, 1 vegetable

Gazpacho

*Use a blender to purée and serve with celery stick for a spiced version
of an alcohol-free Bloody Mary. This may also be used as an appetizer.*

4 SERVINGS

2   cups vegetable juice
½   cup diced tomato
½   cup peeled and diced cucumber
¼   cup diced green pepper
¼   onion, chopped
1   teaspoon lemon juice
1   garlic clove, minced
      Pinch black pepper

Combine all ingredients and purée in a blender. Chill 2 hours and serve.

Prep time: 20 minutes

NUTRITIONAL ANALYSIS PER SERVING:
Serving Size: ¾ cup

Calories:	35	Cholesterol:	0
Protein:	1 g	Fiber:	1 g
Carbohydrate:	8 g	Sodium:	440 mg
Fat:	0	Calcium	18 mg
		Iron	1 mg

Diabetic Exchanges: 1 vegetable

Vegetarian Stew with Ginger

*If you use new red potatoes, you don't have to peel them
before adding them to the broth.*

6 SERVINGS

1   quart water
2   nonfat vegetable stock cubes
6   new red potatoes, washed and cut
     in small cubes
5   raw carrots, peeled and sliced (or
     6 ounces frozen carrots)
1   medium onion, chopped
1   Tablespoon canola or safflower oil
4   ginger snap cookies
2   cups of water
1   15-ounce can of kidney beans (rinsed
     and drained)

Place water and bouillon cubes in a stew pot. Add potatoes and carrots and
start cooking on medium heat. Meanwhile, sauté the chopped onion in oil
in a skillet. Place 4 ginger snaps and 2 cups of water in a blender. Blend on
high speed for about 15 seconds. Add ginger snaps to the onions in the
skillet and cook for about 5 minutes, stirring often. Add this mixture to the
stew pot. Add the kidney beans. Cook for another 20 minutes, or until
potatoes are fully done.

Prep/cook time: 45 minutes

NUTRITIONAL ANALYSIS PER SERVING:
Serving Size: 2 cups

Calories:	200	Cholesterol	0
Protein:	8 g	Fiber:	9 g
Carbohydrate:	35 g	Sodium:	210 mg
Fat:	3 g	Calcium	25 mg
		Iron	1 mg

Diabetic Exchanges: 1 starch, 2 vegetables

Mulligatawny Stew

This is a hearty Indian stew originally made long ago
with British tastes in mind.

4 SERVINGS

5	cups water
3	new red potatoes, with skin, cut in bite-size chunks
3	carrots, peeled and sliced
1	teaspoon olive oil
1	small onion, sliced
2	stalks celery, chopped
2	apples, with skin, cored and cut in wedges
1	Tablespoon flour
1	teaspoon dried parsley
1	Tablespoon curry
1	teaspoon thyme (optional)
½	teaspoon salt
	Pepper to taste

In a large soup pot, put water on to boil. Add the potatoes and carrots to
the water, and cook on medium heat for about 20 minutes. In a skillet,
sauté onions and celery in the oil for a few minutes. Add about a cup of
water from the stew pot to the skillet. Sprinkle with the flour and mix well
to avoid lumps. While the skillet mixture is thickening, cut up and add the
apples. Then add the entire skillet mixture to the stew pot. Add the spices
and simmer 30 minutes or until the potatoes are done and liquid is
reduced to a stew consistency.

Prep/cook time: 1 hour

NUTRITIONAL ANALYSIS PER SERVING:
Serving Size: 1½ cups

Calories:	160	Cholesterol:	0
Protein:	4 g	Fiber:	6 g
Carbohydrate:	33 g	Sodium:	310 mg
Fat:	1 g	Calcium	39 mg
		Iron	1 mg

Diabetic Exchanges: 1 starch, 1 vegetable, 1 fruit

Portuguese Bean Soup

You can buy the vegetables precut to save time, if you like.

6 SERVINGS

4 cups vegetable broth
2 cups water
2 carrots, sliced
2 potatoes, peeled and cut into chunks
½ large onion, chopped
2 bay leaves
1 Tablespoon fresh basil
(or ½ Tablespoon dried)

½ cup bottled sweet-sour sauce
¾ cup tomato juice
1 16-ounce can of pinto beans, rinsed
and drained
½ head cabbage, chopped
Pepper to taste

Combine first 7 ingredients in a soup pot and cook 10 minutes.
Add rest of ingredients. Cook 15 minutes or until vegetables are tender.

Prep/cook time: 50 minutes

NUTRITIONAL ANALYSIS PER SERVING:
Serving Size: 1¾ cups

Calories:	170	Cholesterol	0
Protein:	8 g	Fiber:	9 g
Carbohydrate:	33 g	Sodium:	580 mg
Fat:	2 g	Calcium	103 mg
		Iron	3 mg

Diabetic Exchanges: 1 starch, 2 vegetables

Minestrone Soup

Vary vegetables as you like according to your preference. You may also want to try a homemade spice blend using marjoram or savory, see page 248.

6 SERVINGS

1	small onion, diced
1	Tablespoon olive oil
2	quarts water
1	cup of cut fresh green beans
2	fresh tomatoes, chopped
3	carrots, peeled and sliced
2	potatoes, peeled and diced
	(If using new red potatoes, leave the skin on.)
2	teaspoons fresh basil, or 1 teaspoon dried
½	teaspoon dried oregano
½	teaspoon dried rosemary (or finely chopped fresh)
1	teaspoon salt
	Dash of pepper
1	15-ounce can pinto beans (rinsed and drained), divided
1	cup dry small pasta (such as elbow or small shell)

In a large soup pot, sauté onion in the oil. Add all ingredients except beans and pasta. Add about half of the beans with a cup of the soup water to a blender. Purée and add, with the remaining beans, to the pot. Cook on medium heat for about 15 minutes. Bring to a boil, then reduce heat and add the pasta. Cook another 12 minutes, or until the pasta is done.

Prep/cook time: 50 minutes

NUTRITIONAL ANALYSIS PER SERVING:
Serving Size: 2 cups

Calories:	250	Cholesterol:	0
Protein:	10 g	Fiber:	9 g
Carbohydrate:	48 g	Sodium:	200 mg
Fat:	3 g	Calcium	49 mg
		Iron	3 mg

Diabetic Exchanges: 3 starches, 1 protein, 1 vegetable

Cuban Black Bean Soup

*I suggest serving this with cornbread or another whole-grain bread
for a complete meal.*

6 SERVINGS

1½   cups dry black beans
1   onion, chopped
2   Tablespoons canola oil
6   cups vegetable broth
2   carrots, diced
½   teaspoon cumin
1   Tablespoon soy sauce
1   teaspoon ground ginger (optional)

If possible, soak the beans for 1½ hours (or over-night) in plenty
of water before starting. Rinse.

In a soup pot, sauté the onion in the oil for a minute. Add the broth,
carrots, and cumin. Add the beans and cook until tender (about 2 hours
with soaking, 3 hours without soak). Remove about ½ of the mixture to
purée and return to the pot. Add soy sauce and garnish with scallions,
if desired.

Prep/cook time: 2½ hours, after soaking

NUTRITIONAL ANALYSIS PER SERVING:
Serving Size: 1½ cups

Calories:	220	Cholesterol	0
Protein:	12 g	Fiber:	11 g
Carbohydrate:	32 g	Sodium:	516 mg
Fat:	5 g	Calcium	46 mg
		Iron	3 mg

Diabetic Exchanges: 2 starches, 1 protein, 1 vegetable

Vegetable Barley Soup

*Barley is a grain that can be found in health food stores
or on supermarket shelves with the cereals for cooking. The potatoes can be
microwaved 3 to 4 minutes first to reduce cooking time.*

4 SERVINGS

1	Tablespoon vegetable oil
1	onion, chopped
½	cup sliced fresh mushrooms
1	quart water
½	cup barley
2	large or 3 small potatoes, peeled and chopped
2	carrots, peeled and sliced
1	teaspoon dried basil
½	teaspoon dried rosemary
½	teaspoon salt
1	cup skim milk

In a large soup pot, sauté onion and mushrooms. Add remaining
ingredients except milk and cook 25 to 30 minutes or until potatoes are
tender. Add milk and heat thoroughly without boiling. Season with pepper,
if desired.

Prep/cook time: 45 minutes

NUTRITIONAL ANALYSIS PER SERVING:
Serving Size: 2 cups

Calories:	220	Cholesterol:	1 mg
Protein:	7 g	Fiber:	6 g
Carbohydrate:	40 g	Sodium:	310 mg
Fat:	4 g	Calcium	93 mg
		Iron	1 mg

Diabetic Exchanges: 1 starch, 1 protein, 1 vegetable

Red Lentil Ragout

Use fresh herbs, if possible, in this French-like stew.

4 SERVINGS

2	cups dry red lentils
4	cups water
1	large or 2 small onions, chopped
2	garlic cloves, minced
1	Tablespoon olive oil
2	14-ounce cans vegetable broth
2	cups water
1	cup of cut fresh or frozen green beans
3	carrots, peeled and chopped
2	small new red potatoes, washed and chopped
½	cup burgundy wine
½	teaspoon each of thyme and savory
¼	teaspoon marjoram

In a 2-quart sauce pan, cook the lentils in the 4 cups of water until done, about 40 to 45 minutes. Meanwhile, in a large stew pot, sauté garlic and onion in the oil. Add remaining ingredients and simmer until potatoes are done. Take about half of the potatoes out with a large spoon and purée in a blender with some broth. Return puréed potato to the pot and add more water, if necessary, for a stew-like consistency. Add cooked and drained lentils and mix together.

Prep/cook time: 1 hour

NUTRITIONAL ANALYSIS PER SERVING:
Serving Size: 2 cups

Calories:	220	Cholesterol	0
Protein:	10 g	Fiber:	7 g
Carbohydrate:	35 g	Sodium:	580 mg
Fat:	4 g	Calcium	55 mg
		Iron	3 mg

Diabetic Exchanges: 1 starch, 1 protein, 2 vegetables

Creamy Borscht

This recipe is an excellent source of vitamin A.
If you don't own a food processor or a blender that holds 6 cups, you may have to
purée in sections in the blender before adding to a serving bowl.

4 SERVINGS

3½ cups water
6   cloves garlic, whole
2   carrots, peeled and cut in large chunks
1   teaspoon fresh dill
1   bay leaf

1   16-ounce jar of sliced, pickled beets with juice
¼   cucumber, peeled and chopped
2   cups nonfat vanilla yogurt

In a large soup pot, combine first 5 ingredients for the stock. While the
stock is cooking, combine beets, beet juice, cucumber, and yogurt in a
food processor or blender. Purée. After the stock has been cooking for 20
minutes, remove from the hot burner until warm. You should have at least
2 cups of broth; if not, add more water and heat again. Pour the stock
through a strainer into a large measuring cup and discard the solids. Add 2
cups of the stock to the blender and purée again. Pour the entire blender
contents through the strainer into a serving bowl, stirring as necessary to
get all of the liquid. Chill before serving. Garnish with dill, if desired.

Prep/cook time: 40 minutes

NUTRITIONAL ANALYSIS PER SERVING:
Serving Size: 1½ cups

Calories:	110	Cholesterol:	0
Protein:	5 g	Fiber:	3 g
Carbohydrate:	22 g	Sodium:	340 mg
Fat:	trace	Calcium	83 mg
		Iron	1 mg

Diabetic Exchanges: 1 starch, 1 vegetable

Mexican Corn and Bean Salad

This recipe works well for a box lunch or picnic; it holds up well outdoors without refrigeration and you can double the recipe inexpensively. Serve attractively at home in a tortilla hat (see directions to make below).

6 SERVINGS

Salad:
1   15-ounce can corn, rinsed and drained
1   15-ounce can kidney beans, rinsed and drained
1   cup cubed nonfat Cheddar cheese or soy cheese
¼   cup chopped onion
1   cup chopped celery
1   sweet red or green pepper, diced

Dressing:
1   Tablespoon olive oil
2   Tablespoons lemon juice
1   teaspoon cumin
½   cup Picanté sauce (mild)
1   clove garlic, pressed through garlic press*

Salad: Combine all ingredients together.

Dressing: In a small bowl, mix all dressing ingredients together and add to the salad mixture. Blend and serve chilled.

Tortilla hat: Brush 6 flour tortillas with a little olive oil, using a pastry brush. Place 6 custard cups upside down on a baking sheet and lay the tortillas over the cups, making loose folds. Bake at 400°F until edges are browned, about 10 minutes. **Prep time: 40 minutes**

*Prebake garlic for a milder flavor by baking in tin foil for 15 minutes; mix in Picanté sauce.

NUTRITIONAL ANALYSIS PER SERVING:			
Serving Size: 1 cup			
Calories:	220	Cholesterol	0
Protein:	12 g	Fiber:	9 g
Carbohydrate:	36 g	Sodium:	530 mg
Fat:	3 g	Calcium	170 mg
		Iron	1 mg

Diabetic Exchanges: 2 starches, 1 protein, 1 vegetable

Spanish Three Bean Salad

If you haven't worked with fresh cilantro before, I recommend starting with just a touch of it and add according to taste.

6 SERVINGS

Dressing:
¼   cup water
2   Tablespoons sugar
3   Tablespoons olive oil
3   Tablespoons red wine vinegar
½   teaspoon salt
   Dash of pepper

Salad:
1   16-ounce can each of green beans, small white beans, kidney beans (rinsed and drained)
1   red bell pepper, diced
3   scallions, thinly sliced (or ½ cup chopped onion
1   Tablespoon loosely packed cilantro leaves, finely chopped

Mix dressing in a large serving bowl. Add remaining ingredients and toss to mix. Chill a day before serving so flavors blend, if so desired.

Prep time: 30 minutes

NUTRITIONAL ANALYSIS PER SERVING:
Serving Size: 1 cup

Calories:	290	Cholesterol:	0
Protein:	13 g	Fiber:	15 g
Carbohydrate:	46 g	Sodium:	370 mg
Fat:	7 g	Calcium	77 mg
		Iron	3 mg

Diabetic Exchanges: 2 starches, 1 protein, 1 vegetable, 1 fat

Spinach Salad

This variation contains potatoes, a reduced fat alternative to croutons.

4 SERVINGS

2	hard boiled egg whites
1½	cups diced or cubed potatoes (frozen or fresh)
1	Tablespoon olive oil
½	cup vegetable broth
1	Tablespoon dried parsley
1	10-ounce package of fresh spinach, washed
¼	large red onion, thinly sliced
1	Tablespoon imitation bacon bits (soy-based)

Start the water to boil 2 eggs. When the eggs are hard boiled, peel and cool. Discard yolks.

Sauté the potatoes in the oil until the oil is absorbed. Add broth and parsley and continue cooking until potatoes are done. Remove potatoes to a plate and cool potatoes along with egg whites.

Cut the spinach, discarding ends and bad spots. Place in a large bowl; add all other ingredients. Toss with a nonfat vinaigrette.

Prep/cook time: 45 minutes

NUTRITIONAL ANALYSIS PER SERVING, WITH 2 TABLESPOONS DRESSING:
Serving Size: 1 cup

Calories:	130	Cholesterol	0
Protein:	7 g	Fiber:	3 g
Carbohydrate:	16 g	Sodium:	450 mg
Fat:	4 g	Calcium	84 mg
		Iron	2 mg

Diabetic Exchanges: 1 starch, 1 vegetable

Spinach and Pomegranate Salad

This side dish is a simple variation of the traditional spinach salad.
Add mandarin oranges, if desired.

6 SERVINGS

Salad:

1	10-ounce bag of fresh spinach, washed and cut in bite-size pieces
½	of a pomegranate, seeds only
2	Tablespoons of freeze-dried cranberries (or ¼ cup frozen berries)
½	red onion, thinly sliced

Dressing:

2	Tablespoons olive oil
1	Tablespoon balsamic vinegar
	Juice of ½ lemon (2 Tablespoons)
1	teaspoon sugar
¼	teaspoon salt
	Pepper to taste

Pick over the spinach, cutting ends and discarding bad leaves.
Add pomegranate seeds, cranberries, and red onion.

Mix dressing ingredients in a small bowl. Pour over spinach mixture and
toss to coat.

Prep time: 30 minutes

NUTRITIONAL ANALYSIS PER SERVING:
Serving Size: ⅔ cup

Calories:	70	Cholesterol:	0
Protein:	1 g	Fiber:	2 g
Carbohydrate:	6 g	Sodium:	120 mg
Fat:	5 g	Calcium	37 mg
		Iron	1 mg

Diabetic Exchanges: 1 vegetable, 1 fat

Summer Romaine Salad

This salad is wonderful for lunch on a hot summer day,
or serve as a simple side dish.

2 SERVINGS

Salad:

Large bunch of romaine lettuce leaves,
cleaned and cut

1   medium tomato, sliced

¼   red onion, sliced very thin

1   hard boiled egg white, chopped

Dressing:

2   teaspoons olive oil

1   teaspoon red wine vinegar

Juice of ½ small lemon

¼   teaspoon salt

Dash of pepper

¼   cup sunflower seeds (optional)

Place romaine, tomato, red onion, and boiled egg white in a large bowl.
In a small bowl, mix olive oil, vinegar, lemon juice, salt and pepper until
blended. Pour over lettuce mixture and toss well. Chill. May be sprinkled
with sunflower seeds, if desired.

Prep time: 25 minutes

NUTRITIONAL ANALYSIS PER SERVING:
Serving Size: 1½ cups

Calories:	75	Cholesterol	0
Protein:	3 g	Fiber:	2 g
Carbohydrate:	7 g	Sodium:	300 mg
Fat:	4 g	Calcium	27 mg
		Iron	1 mg

Diabetic Exchanges: 1 vegetable, 1 fat

Easy Potato Salad

Although always a popular picnic item, you don't need an excuse
to enjoy a healthy potato salad anytime for lunch.

4 SERVINGS

6	small red potatoes (skin on)
½	cup chopped green pepper
¼	cup reduced-calorie mayonnaise
2	Tablespoons Dijon mustard
4	hard boiled egg whites
¼	cup plain nonfat yogurt

Pierce potatoes with a fork and microwave for about 6 to 8 minutes or until
they can are fully cooked. Cut into quarters when cooled. While potatoes
are cooling, combine all other ingredients together. Add potatoes, mixing
well. Serve cold.

Prep/cook time: 30 minutes

NUTRITIONAL ANALYSIS PER SERVING:
Serving Size: ¾ cups

Calories:	170	Cholesterol:	5 mg
Protein:	7 g	Fiber:	2 g
Carbohydrate:	28 g	Sodium:	300 mg
Fat:	3 g	Calcium	45 mg
		Iron	1 mg

Diabetic Exchanges: 1 starch, 1 protein, 1 vegetable

Autumn Rice Salad

Serve this salad cold over a bed of lettuce. Precook the rice before you begin.
Any type of rice (white, brown, or wild) works well in this recipe.

6 SERVINGS

Salad:
4 cups cooked brown rice
1 raw carrot, quartered and chopped
  in small pieces
⅔ cup cooked corn
¼ cup slivered red cabbage
¼ cup cooked black beans

Dressing:
2 Tablespoons sesame or olive oil
2 Tablespoons apple cider vinegar
2 Tablespoons water
2 Tablespoons lemon juice
1 Tablespoon soy sauce
1 small clove fresh garlic, minced
½ teaspoon basil
½ teaspoon oregano
1 Tablespoon fresh parsley,
  for garnish (optional)

In a large bowl, mix together the five salad ingredients. In a blender,
combine all dressing ingredients together, except the parsley. Blend until
smooth. Pour dressing over the salad and garnish with parsley,
if desired. Chill.

Prep time: 30 minutes (with precooked rice)

NUTRITIONAL ANALYSIS PER SERVING:
Serving Size: ¾ cup

Calories:	190	Cholesterol	0
Protein:	4 g	Fiber:	4 g
Carbohydrate:	30 g	Sodium:	150 mg
Fat:	6 g	Calcium	18 mg
		Iron	1 mg

Diabetic Exchanges: 2 starches, 1 fat

Peanutty Rice Salad

This salad can be eaten either hot or cold and it travels well, making it ideal for a brown bag lunch. Use leftover rice, if available, to reduce preparation time.

4 SERVINGS

1   cup dry rice (or 3 cups cooked and cooled)
2   cups water
1   clove garlic, crushed
1   Tablespoon sesame or olive oil
½   cup vegetable broth
2   Tablespoons peanut butter
1   Tablespoon soy sauce
1   teaspoon lemon juice
1   teaspoon fresh ginger
6-7 fresh mushrooms, sliced
4-5 scallions, chopped

Cook rice separately in 2 cups of water; remove from heat and set aside. In a large skillet, sauté the garlic in oil for a minute. Add remaining ingredients, stirring continuously. Cook for 5 to 7 minutes. Remove from heat and cool a bit. Add the rice to the peanut-soy mixture and serve— warm or cold.

Prep/cook time: 40 minutes

NUTRITIONAL ANALYSIS PER SERVING:
Serving Size: 1 cup

Calories:	260	Cholesterol:	0
Protein:	6 g	Fiber:	2 g
Carbohydrate:	41 g	Sodium:	170 mg
Fat:	8 g	Calcium	18 mg
		Iron	3 mg

Diabetic Exchanges: 1 starch, 1 vegetable, 1 fat

Couscous Salad

This dish travels well and can be made in advance.
Carrots can be substituted for the cucumber as a variation.

3 SERVINGS

Salad:

1   cup couscous
1½ cups boiling water
3   stalks celery, chopped
½   green pepper, chopped
½   cucumber, sliced and cut into quarters

Dressing:

2   Tablespoons olive oil
2   Tablespoons vinegar (wine or balsamic)
½   teaspoon crushed garlic
1   Tablespoon dried parsley
½   teaspoon cumin (optional)
½   teaspoon salt
    Dash of pepper

In a large bowl, add couscous to boiling water. Let stand about 20 minutes.
Meanwhile, chop the vegetables and add to the couscous. Make a dressing
of the remaining ingredients and add to the couscous-vegetable mixture.
Mix well and serve chilled.

Prep time: 40 minutes

NUTRITIONAL ANALYSIS PER SERVING:			
Serving Size: ⅔ cup			
Calories:	120	Cholesterol	0
Protein:	2 g	Fiber:	2 g
Carbohydrate:	14 g	Sodium:	290 mg
Fat:	7 g	Calcium	22 mg
		Iron	1 mg

Diabetic Exchanges: 1 starch, 1 fat

Couscous Chick Pea Salad

*This salad can be served on a bed a lettuce or generously stuffed
into pita bread halves.*

4 SERVINGS

1	box couscous (1 cup dry)
1	15-ounce can chick peas,* rinsed and drained
1	red bell pepper, chopped
2	Tablespoons chopped fresh parsley
1	cucumber, peeled, sliced and quartered
2	medium tomatoes, chopped
1	grated carrot (optional)
¼	teaspoon salt
	Pepper to taste
½	cup nonfat Italian dressing

Prepare couscous according to package directions. In a medium bowl,
combine couscous with all ingredients, except Italian dressing. Coat with
nonfat Italian dressing and toss to blend. Serve chilled.

*For an alternative to the chick peas, try black beans with 1 teaspoon cumin.

Prep time: 40 minutes

NUTRITIONAL ANALYSIS PER SERVING WITH 2 TABLESPOONS DRESSING:
Serving Size: 1 cup

Calories:	170	Cholesterol:	0
Protein:	7 g	Fiber:	8 g
Carbohydrate:	32 g	Sodium:	380 mg
Fat:	2 g	Calcium	41 mg
		Iron	1 mg

Diabetic Exchanges: 1 starch, 1 protein, 1 vegetable

Chapter 7

Main Dish: Bean & Legume

Main Dish: Bean & Legume

Marinades & Sauces

Boston Baked Beans

Serve with cornbread for a filling meal. Whether you use the crockpot or oven, you may want to check the beans about an hour before they are done to stir and check for adequate sauce.

9 CUPS / 12 SERVINGS

1	pound dry pinto beans
3	cups of water (or a little more, if needed)
1	small onion, chopped
1	Tablespoon vegetable oil
1	8-ounce can tomato sauce
¼	cup molasses
½	cup brown sugar
1	Tablespoon dry mustard
2	Tablespoons Worcestershire sauce
½	teaspoon salt

In a large saucepan, cover beans with plenty of water and soak over-night or about 12 hours. Drain beans the following day. Rinse with more water and drain again. Add the 3 cups of water and a few drops of Beano® here, if desired.

Crockpot method: Combine the beans with water in the crockpot. Add the remaining ingredients to the crockpot. Cook on high setting for about 5½ to 6 hours.

Casserole method: Combine the beans with water in a large casserole dish. Mix in remaining ingredients. Cover and bake for about 4 hours at 325°F.

In either method, check beans near the end to make sure they are tender and the sauce has thickened.

Prep/cook time: 5-6 hours

NUTRITIONAL ANALYSIS PER SERVING:
Serving Size: ¾ cup

Calories:	190	Cholesterol:	0
Protein:	8 g	Fiber:	8 g
Carbohydrate:	37 g	Sodium:	340 mg
Fat:	1 g	Calcium	72 mg
		Iron	3 mg

Diabetic Exchanges: 1 starch, 1 protein, 1 vegetable

Vegetarian Chili

This recipe can be prepared ahead and warmed in a crockpot.

6 CUPS / 4 SERVINGS

½   cup chopped onion
1   clove garlic, minced
¼   cup dry vermouth or white wine
1   Tablespoon chili powder
1   teaspoon basil
¼   teaspoon oregano
¼   teaspoon cumin
½   teaspoon salt
1   cup finely chopped zucchini
1   cup finely chopped carrots
1   28-ounce can tomatoes, drained and chopped
1   cup cooked kidney beans, rinsed and drained
1   cup water, approximately

In a large pot, sauté onions and garlic in wine until soft. Mix in spices. Add zucchini and carrots and cook for a few minutes over low heat, stirring occasionally. Stir in tomatoes and beans. Bring to a boil; then reduce heat and simmer for 30 to 40 minutes, adding water to desired consistency.

Prep/cook time: 1 hour

NUTRITIONAL ANALYSIS PER SERVING:
Serving Size: 1½ cups

Calories:	230	Cholesterol:	0
Protein:	13 g	Fiber:	12 g
Carbohydrate:	42 g	Sodium:	340 mg
Fat:	1 g	Calcium	86 mg
		Iron	3 mg

Diabetic Exchanges: 1 starch, 1 protein, 2 vegetables

Bean Burritos

*These burritos are baked, but can be made on top of the stove by placing the fill-
ing into a warmed tortilla; wrap and serve. Two of these makes a hearty supper.*

12 BURRITOS / 6 SERVINGS

1	large white onion, chopped
2	cups chopped green peppers
1	Tablespoon olive oil
2	cups of cooked pinto beans, rinsed and drained
1	cup frozen corn
2	cups Salsa (page 49) or mild Picanté sauce, divided
4	tomatoes, chopped, divided
1	cup shredded nonfat Cheddar cheese, divided
12	flour tortillas

In a skillet, sauté the onion and green pepper in the oil. Add the pinto
beans, corn, and ½ of the salsa. Cook for a few minutes, then remove from
the heat. Add ½ of the tomatoes and ½ of the cheese to the bean mixture;
stir well.

Spoon ½ cup of the bean mixture onto each tortilla. Roll up and place (edge
side down) in a nonstick baking dish. Cover with remaining salsa; sprinkle
with remaining cheese.

Bake for 20 minutes in preheated 400°F oven. Top with remainder of fresh
tomatoes on the plate. Serve immediately.

Prep/cook time: 50 minutes

NUTRITIONAL ANALYSIS PER SERVING:
Serving Size: 2 burritos

Calories:	420	Cholesterol:	5 mg
Protein:	18 g	Fiber:	10 g
Carbohydrate:	71 g	Sodium:	830 mg
Fat:	7 g	Calcium	276 mg
		Iron	5 mg

Diabetic Exchanges: 3 starches, 1 protein, 2 vegetables, 1 fat

Italian Beans and Rice

*Italy is known for its pasta dishes, but Northern Italians actually eat a lot
of rice. The key to this recipe is a fresh, good quality Marinara sauce,
which can be purchased at a specialty store or large supermarket.
You can also make your own Marinara Sauce on page 52.*

4 ½ CUPS / 3 SERVINGS

1   onion, chopped
2   cloves garlic, crushed
2   teaspoons olive oil
1   cup arborio or short grain rice, uncooked
2½   cups warm water
1   cup fresh Marinara Sauce (page 52)
¾   cup of canned cannelini (or similar) beans,
      rinsed and drained
1   Tablespoon fresh basil (or ½ Tablespoon
      dried)
⅛   teaspoon crushed red pepper

Chop the onion and crush garlic. Sauté in the oil in a saucepan for a
minute. Add the uncooked rice and cook for another minute. Add 1 cup of
the water and cook, uncovered, stirring occasionally, until water is half
evaporated. Add remainder of water and cook until rice is done
(about 15 minutes).

Meanwhile, rinse and drain the beans. When the rice is done, add the
sauce, beans, basil, and pepper. Heat thoroughly and serve.

Prep/cook time: 40 minutes

NUTRITIONAL ANALYSIS PER SERVING:
Serving Size: 1½ cups

Calories:	360	Cholesterol:	0
Protein:	9 g	Fiber:	5 g
Carbohydrate:	67 g	Sodium:	460 mg
Fat:	6 g	Calcium	32 mg
		Iron	3 mg

Diabetic Exchanges: 3 starches, 1 protein, 1 vegetable, 1 fat

Moro's Caribbean Beans and Rice

This variation of beans and rice contains a decent amount of cilantro.
If you've never tried it, use it sparingly at first.

6 CUPS / 4 SERVINGS

1   Tablespoon olive oil
1   green pepper, sliced
1   medium onion, sliced
2   cloves garlic, minced
1   Tablespoon tomato paste
4   cups water
1½ cups long grain rice, uncooked
1   teaspoon oregano
¼   teaspoon salt
4   sprigs fresh cilantro
1   16-ounce can of beans (kidney or pinto),
    rinsed and drained

In a large saucepan, sauté the pepper, onion and garlic in the oil for
2 minutes. Add remaining ingredients. Simmer, covered, until rice is done.
Season with pepper, if you like.

Prep/cook time: 45 minutes

NUTRITIONAL ANALYSIS PER SERVING:
Serving Size: 1½ cups

Calories:	310	Cholesterol:	0
Protein:	6 g	Fiber:	3 g
Carbohydrate:	62 g	Sodium:	140 mg
Fat:	4 g	Calcium	54 mg
		Iron	6 mg

Diabetic Exchanges: 3 starches, 1 protein, 1 vegetable

Spanish Beans and Rice

*This is a variation of a recipe which originates in the Dominican Republic.
Racaito sauce is a sweet pepper condiment with added flavorings. It can be
found in the Spanish section of the supermarket, near the salsa. If unavailable,
you can use any pepper sauce, spicy or sweet.*

5 CUPS / 3 SERVINGS

1	cup rice, uncooked
2	cups water
1	teaspoon olive oil
¼	cup chopped onion
1	cup of canned (or fresh) chopped tomatoes
1	cup of canned kidney or pinto beans, drained
1	teaspoon oregano
1	Tablespoon Racaito sauce
1	Tablespoon salsa or Picanté sauce (optional)
½	teaspoon salt
	Pepper to taste

Measure 2 cups of water in a saucepan. Heat water to boiling, add rice and
cook, covered. In a skillet, sauté the onion in oil for a minute; then add the
remaining ingredients. When the rice is fully cooked, add rice to the bean
mixture and mix thoroughly.

Prep/cook time: 40 minutes

NUTRITIONAL ANALYSIS PER SERVING:
Serving Size: 1⅔ cups

Calories:	330	Cholesterol:	0
Protein:	10 g	Fiber:	7 g
Carbohydrate:	68 g	Sodium:	380 mg
Fat:	2 g	Calcium:	51 mg
		Iron	5 mg

Diabetic Exchanges: 3 starches, 1 protein, 1 vegetable

Brazilian Black Beans and Rice

This is a good recipe for days when you're home early; it's simple, but takes 2½ hours to cook. Pinto beans can be substituted for the black beans.

8 CUPS / 4 SERVINGS

1¼	cups dry black beans
4	cups water
4	cloves garlic, whole
1	onion, whole
1	cup chopped onion (1 large)
1	sweet green pepper, chopped
1	clove garlic, minced
½	teaspoon salt
1	cup long grain rice, uncooked
2	cups water
	Nonfat cooking spray

In a large saucepan, cover the beans in plenty of water. Soak over night or about 12 hours. Then bring the beans to a boil with 4 cups of fresh water. Reduce heat, add whole garlic and whole onion; cook 2 hours. During the last 30 minutes, start the water boiling for the rice.

In a skillet coated with cooking spray, sauté the chopped onion and green pepper. Add minced garlic and salt.

When the beans are done, remove the whole cloves of garlic and onion and add the beans to the skillet mixture. Blend for a few minutes.

Serve over rice and top with your favorite salsa, either prepared or with a homemade recipe (see page 49).

Prep/cook time: 2½ hours

NUTRITIONAL ANALYSIS PER SERVING, WITH RICE:
Serving Size: 2 cups

Calories:	380	Cholesterol:	0
Protein:	17 g	Fiber:	14 g
Carbohydrate:	76 g	Sodium:	270 mg
Fat:	1 g	Calcium	62 mg
		Iron	5 mg

Diabetic Exchanges: 3 starches, 1 protein, 1 vegetable

Tamale Pie

If so desired, make this pie spicier by using the "medium-hot" Picanté sauce or adding ⅛ teaspoon of cayenne pepper. This is a hearty dish for good appetites.

9 X 13-INCH BAKING DISH / 8 PORTIONS

Vegetable filling:

1	Tablespoon olive oil or canola oil
1	medium onion, chopped
1	16-ounce jar mild Picanté sauce
1	15-ounce can crushed tomatoes
1	10-ounce bag frozen corn
1	16-ounce can pinto beans, rinsed and drained
1	teaspoon cumin

Cornmeal crust:

1¼	cups skim milk
1	cup cornmeal
2	teaspoons oil
1	teaspoon baking powder
2	Tablespoons sugar
½	teaspoon salt
¼	cup nonfat egg substitute
1¼	cups flour

Vegetable filling: In a skillet, sauté the onion in oil. Add remaining ingredients and simmer while making the cornmeal crust.

Cornmeal crust: In a saucepan, heat milk until hot, but not boiling. Turn off the heat but leave saucepan on the burner. Add cornmeal slowly, stirring continuously, to avoid clumping. Whisk until it starts to thicken. Mix in remaining ingredients, adding the flour slowly. You should have a muffin batter consistency. *(continued on next page)*

NUTRITIONAL ANALYSIS PER SERVING:
Serving Size: 1 portion

Calories:	330	Cholesterol:	0
Protein:	12 g	Fiber:	8 g
Carbohydrate:	61 g	Sodium:	610 mg
Fat:	4 g	Calcium	113 mg
		Iron	4 mg

Diabetic Exchanges: 3 starches, 1 protein, 1 vegetable

Place the vegetable mixture on the bottom of a 9 x 13-inch square baking dish or 2½-quart casserole dish. Top with the cornmeal mixture.

Bake at 350°F for 30 minutes, or until the cornbread turns golden brown on the edges.

Prep/cook time: 1 hour

Hummus

This recipe can be used as a sandwich spread for pita halves,
or used as a snack on pita triangles.

2 ½ CUPS / 10 SERVINGS

2	cups cooked chick peas (drain liquid if canned), divided
2	Tablespoons lemon juice
⅔	cup water
1	Tablespoon olive oil
1	Tablespoon soy sauce
½	teaspoon garlic powder
1	Tablespoon dried parsley
1	small onion, chopped
½	teaspoon salt
½	teaspoon pepper
½	teaspoon cumin (optional)

In a blender, combine 1 cup chick peas with remaining ingredients and blend until mashed. Add remaining chick peas to make a soft paste-like consistency. If too thin, add more chick peas; if too thick, add more water. Serve chilled.

Prep time: 30 minutes

NUTRITIONAL ANALYSIS PER SERVING:
Serving Size: 1/4 cup

Calories:	70	Cholesterol:	0
Protein:	3 g	Fiber:	2 g
Carbohydrate:	10 g	Sodium:	160 mg
Fat:	2 g	Calcium	19 mg
		Iron	1 mg

Diabetic Exchanges: 1 starch

Shepherd's Pie

If you really like the idea of meat, potato and vegetable all in one dish, this is your casserole. There are a few steps involved, but the result is a satisfying meal.

8-INCH SQUARE BAKING DISH / 6 PORTIONS

Meat substitute layer:
1 cup TVP® granules
2 cups very hot water
3-4 cloves garlic, minced
1 Tablespoon olive oil
1 Tablespoon light soy sauce
2 Tablespoons catsup

Vegetable layer:
1 medium onion, chopped
1½ cups vegetable broth
2 cups frozen corn
1 cup frozen sliced carrots
½ teaspoon marjoram or thyme
1 teaspoon olive oil
2 Tablespoons flour

Potato layer:
4 large potatoes, peeled
⅓ cup skim milk
½ teaspoon salt

In a mixing bowl, soak the TVP® in the hot water for 20 minutes. Meanwhile, cook the potatoes in a large saucepan.

Meat substitute layer: Sauté the garlic in the oil in a large skillet for a minute; then add the TVP®, soy sauce, and catsup. Cook for about 15 minutes, stirring occasionally. *(continued on next page)*

(continued on next page)

NUTRITIONAL ANALYSIS PER SERVING:
Serving Size: 1 portion

Calories:	270	Cholesterol:	0
Protein:	18 g	Fiber:	8 g
Carbohydrate:	43 g	Sodium:	430 mg
Fat:	3 g	Calcium	37 mg
		Iron	1 mg

Diabetic Exchanges: 2 starches, 1 protein, 2 vegetables

While the TVP® is cooking, chop the onion and set aside. In a mixing bowl, combine broth, corn, carrots, and marjoram. When the TVP® is cooked, spoon this mixture into an 8-inch square baking dish that is at least 3 inches deep.

Vegetable layer: Use large skillet to sauté the onion in the olive oil. Add the corn-broth mixture to onion and sprinkle with flour. Stir and cook until the sauce is thickened (about 10 minutes). Spoon this mixture over the meat substitute layer in baking dish.

Potato layer: Drain the cooked potatoes and mash with the milk and salt. Spread mashed potatoes over top to cover vegetables. Bake for 30 minutes at 350°F.

Vegetarian Jambalaya

Enjoy the unique flavors of Cajun cooking without the meat.
Cayenne pepper is a hot spice that seems to get hotter with simmering time. If
you're unsure how spicy to make it, you can always start with the amount listed,
test the sauce at the end of the cooking time, and add more, if desired.

6 CUPS / 3 SERVINGS

2	soy-based sausage links, cut in bite-sized chunks
1	medium onion, sliced
1	Tablespoon olive oil
1	large sweet red pepper, sliced
1	large sweet green pepper, sliced
1	28-ounce can chopped tomatoes
½	cup cooked black-eyed peas or pinto beans*
1	Tablespoon Worcestershire sauce
½	teaspoon oregano
2	bay leaves
⅛	teaspoon cayenne pepper
1	cup uncooked rice
2	cups water

In a large stir-fry pan, sauté soy sausages and onion in the oil for 5 minutes. Add sliced peppers and remaining ingredients, except the rice, to the stir-fry pan. Turn heat to low, cover, and simmer for 35 to 40 minutes. Meanwhile, add 2 cups of water to a saucepan and start heating to a boil for the rice. Add rice. Reduce heat and cook the rice; remove the bay leaves from the vegetable mixture. Serve the jambalaya over the cooked rice.

*If starting with dry beans, cook according to the package directions. If using canned beans, just rinse and drain. You may want to cook them the day before to save time.

Prep/cook time: 50 minutes

NUTRITIONAL ANALYSIS PER SERVING:
Serving Size: 2 cups

Calories:	320	Cholesterol:	0
Protein:	10 g	Fiber:	5 g
Carbohydrate:	59 g	Sodium:	370 mg
Fat:	5 g	Calcium:	130 mg
		Iron	4 mg

Diabetic Exchanges: 2 starches, 1 protein, 2 vegetables

Easy Lentil Casserole

*Orange juice enlivens this simple, nutritious recipe. I use a homemade stock
with about a half teaspoon of salt added. If using canned stock,
dilute with additional water.*

6 CUPS / 4 SERVINGS

6	cups dry lentils
1	cup brown rice, uncooked
1	cup frozen sliced carrots
3	cups vegetable stock
1	cup orange juice
1	teaspoon canola or safflower oil
1	Tablespoon parsley
1	teaspoon cumin

In a large casserole dish, combine all ingredients. Bake at 350°F for approximately 2 to 2½ hours, or until lentils are done.

Stir and check liquid level after 1½ hours.

Prep/cook time: 2½ hours

NUTRITIONAL ANALYSIS PER SERVING:
Serving Size: 1 ½ cups

Calories:	340	Cholesterol:	0
Protein:	14 g	Fiber:	7 g
Carbohydrate:	65 g	Sodium:	350 mg
Fat:	3 g	Calcium	43 mg
		Iron	4 mg

Diabetic Exchanges: 3 starches, 1 protein, 1 vegetable

Stuffed Peppers

Prepare Lentil Tomato Sauce on page 53, ahead of time to top these peppers.

6 STUFFED PEPPERS

6	large green peppers
1	medium onion, finely chopped
½	cup white wine
1	clove garlic, minced
1½	cups chopped tomatoes
2½	cups sliced mushrooms (about ½ pound)
2	Tablespoons fresh basil
½	Tablespoon oregano
1	Tablespoon low-sodium tamari or soy sauce
1½	cups cooked brown rice
	Lentil Tomato Sauce (page 53)

Remove the tops and seeds from the green peppers and set aside. In skillet, sauté onions in wine until translucent. Add garlic and tomatoes, stirring until tomato pieces lose their shape. Add mushrooms, spices and tamari. Cook until mushrooms are tender. Stir in rice, then place stuffing into peppers. Arrange peppers in colander and place the colander in soup kettle with one or two inches of water. Steam stuffed peppers until tender, about 20 minutes. Serve immediately with Lentil Tomato Sauce (see page 53) or Marinara Sauce (see page 52).

Prep/cook time: 45 minutes

NUTRITIONAL ANALYSIS PER SERVING, WITHOUT THE SAUCE:
Serving Size: 1 stuffed pepper

Calories:	120	Cholesterol:	0
Protein:	5 g	Fiber:	4 g
Carbohydrate:	23 g	Sodium:	95 mg
Fat:	1 g	Calcium	34 mg
		Iron	2 mg

Diabetic Exchanges: 1 starch, 1 vegetable

Lentils with Mixed Peppers

It's worth the added expense to use red peppers which add sweetness and color to this healthy, high-fiber main dish. This dish travels well as a bag lunch.

6 CUPS / 4 SERVINGS

2	teaspoons olive oil
1	medium onion, diced
1	red pepper, cut in thin strips
1	green pepper, cut in thin strips
2	small cloves garlic, minced
3	cups vegetable broth*
	(or 3 cups water with one bouillon cube)
½	cup dry lentils
1	cup dry rice, uncooked

In a skillet, sauté the vegetables and garlic in oil until tender. Add the broth and lentils; simmer for 15 minutes. Reduce heat and add rice. Cook on low heat about 30 minutes or until rice is done.

If desired, top with nonfat sour cream.

*Commercial canned vegetable broths are very high in sodium. If you do use them, try adding only one can and diluting with water. Homemade Vegetable Broth (see page 65) is best if you have the time to make it in advance.

Prep/cook time: 1 hour

NUTRITIONAL ANALYSIS PER SERVING:
Serving Size: 1½ cups

Calories:	300	Cholesterol:	0
Protein:	11 g	Fiber:	5 g
Carbohydrate:	57 g	Sodium:	360 mg
Fat:	3 g	Calcium	39 mg
		Iron	4 mg

Diabetic Exchanges: 3 starches, 1 protein, 1 vegetable

Veggie-Lentil Casserole

Use fresh herbs if possible but dried will work, too.

7½ CUPS / 6 SERVINGS

2	cups chopped vegetables*
2	cups cooked lentils
½	cup cooked oatmeal
½	cup lowfat shredded Cheddar cheese
2	Tablespoons soy sauce
1	teaspoon fresh oregano (or ½ teaspoon dried)
¼	cup fresh chopped parsley
1	teaspoon fresh thyme (or ½ teaspoon dried)
½	teaspoon pepper
3	cups breadcrumbs or leftover bread, finely chopped
	Nonfat cooking spray

Preheat oven to 400°F. Spray 2-quart casserole dish with cooking spray. Precook the vegetables, lentils and oatmeal (according to package directions). In large bowl, combine all ingredients. Mix well. Place mixture in a 2-quart baking dish, cover and bake for 20 minutes at 400°F.

* You can use any combo of onion/mushroom/carrot/celery/broccoli. Sauté the onion in a teaspoon of oil, then add vegetables (with ¼ cup wine or broth) and simmer for 10 minutes. Adding frozen, precut, carrots or broccoli will save time; leftover vegetables work well, too.

Prep/cook time: 45 minutes

NUTRITIONAL ANALYSIS PER SERVING:
Serving Size: 1¼ cups

Calories:	220	Cholesterol:	5 mg
Protein:	15 g	Fiber:	7 g
Carbohydrate:	36 g	Sodium:	310 mg
Fat:	2 g	Calcium	215 mg
		Iron	6 mg

Diabetic Exchanges: 2 starches, 1 protein, 1 vegetable

Simple Curried Rice

*This dish can be reheated as a brown bag lunch in either
the microwave or toaster oven.*

6 CUPS / 4 SERVINGS

½   cup dry red lentils (or yellow split peas)
1   cup rice, uncooked, preferably basmati
1   Tablespoon olive oil
1   large onion, sliced
2¼ cups vegetable broth, divided
2   teaspoons curry
½   teaspoon cardamom (optional)

In a small saucepan, cook the lentils according to package directions.

In a separate large saucepan, combine rice, oil, and onion; heat for
2 minutes, stirring constantly. Add half the broth and boil for 5 minutes,
adding spices. Add remaining broth; reduce heat, cover, and simmer
another 15 to 20 minutes or until rice is cooked. Add lentils to rice mixture
and stir gently.

Prep/cook time: 45 minutes

NUTRITIONAL ANALYSIS PER SERVING:
Serving Size: 1½ cups

Calories:	290	Cholesterol:	0
Protein:	11 g	Fiber:	4 g
Carbohydrate:	53 g	Sodium:	250 mg
Fat:	4 g	Calcium	31 mg
		Iron	4 mg

Diabetic Exchanges: 2 starches, 1 protein, 1 vegetable

Pad-Thai

Don't let the exotic name throw you. The ingredients are familiar and easy to find. To save time, buy cabbage already shredded.

9 CUPS / 6 SERVINGS

8   ounces uncooked angel hair pasta

2   cloves garlic, crushed
1   teaspoon olive oil*
½   cup vegetable broth
2   cups cabbage, shredded
2   cups fresh bean sprouts
2-3 scallions, chopped
1   teaspoon ground ginger
1   teaspoon dried basil (or 2 teaspoons fresh)
½   cup dry roasted peanuts, chopped
1   Tablespoon olive oil
1   Tablespoon soy sauce

Put a pot of water on to boil for the pasta and fully cook the pasta separately. In a skillet, sauté the garlic in 1 teaspoon of oil for a minute; then add broth, vegetables and spices. While pasta and vegetables are cooking, chop the peanuts in a blender. Add them to the cooked vegetables.

Drain the cooked pasta and place in a serving bowl. Add 1 Tablespoon of oil and the soy sauce; toss well to coat.

Add the vegetables to the pasta. Mix well and serve either hot or cold.

*Can substitute with hot chili pepper oil.

Prep/cook time: 35 minutes

NUTRITIONAL ANALYSIS PER SERVING: *Serving Size: 1½ cups*			
Calories:	260	Cholesterol:	0
Protein:	10 g	Fiber:	3 g
Carbohydrate:	35 g	Sodium:	150 mg
Fat:	10 g	Calcium	30 mg
		Iron	2 mg

Diabetic Exchanges: 2 starches, 1 protein, 1 vegetable, 1 fat

Subgum Chow Mein

Use a good quality soy sauce or tamari sauce for a recipe like this where the sauce predominates.

4 CUPS / 4 SERVINGS

2 teaspoons olive or sesame oil
4-5 stalks celery, sliced
2 medium or 1 large onion, sliced
⅔ cup vegetable broth or nonfat bouillon with water
3 cups fresh bean sprouts
6-7 fresh mushrooms, chopped
3 Tablespoons light soy sauce
1 Tablespoon cornstarch
2 teaspoons sugar
⅓ cup water
¼ cup unsalted dry roasted peanuts

In a skillet, sauté celery and onion in the oil. Add broth, bean sprouts, mushrooms, and soy sauce. Cook until vegetables are done. Combine cornstarch, sugar and water. Add to the vegetable mixture and heat until thickened. Add peanuts. Serve over rice.

Prep/cook time: 30 minutes

NUTRITIONAL ANALYSIS PER SERVING:
Serving Size: 1 cup

Calories:	150	Cholesterol:	0
Protein:	7 g	Fiber:	4 g
Carbohydrate:	17 g	Sodium:	580 mg
Fat:	6 g	Calcium	47 mg
		Iron	2 mg

Diabetic Exchanges: 1 protein, 2 vegetables, 1 fat

Veggie Burritos with Black Bean Sauce

This is a tomato-free, mildly spiced version of the popular Mexican dish.

6 BURRITOS / 6 SERVINGS

Sauce:

1	Tablespoon olive oil
1	teaspoon prepared minced garlic
¼	cup red pepper, chopped
1	15-ounce can black beans, drained and rinsed
⅓	cup water
1	Tablespoon soy sauce or tamari
½	teaspoon cilantro, chopped

Filling:

½	cup vegetable broth
1	onion, chopped
1	cup sliced mushrooms
2	carrots, shredded or diced
1	cup broccoli, chopped
1	red pepper, chopped
1	cup fresh mung bean sprouts
6	flour tortillas

To make the sauce: In a skillet, sauté the garlic and red pepper in the oil for a few minutes. Then add beans and water. Top with soy sauce and cilantro and set aside. *To make the filling:* In a saucepan, simmer all vegetables in the broth for about 5 minutes, adding more broth if necessary.
To assemble: Warm tortillas by either placing them in the oven (covered with foil) or placing them on a cooling rack over the skillet as the vegetables are simmering. Add about 3 tablespoons of filling to each. Roll and place, edges down, on a plate. Spoon warm sauce over each tortilla and serve. **Prep/cook time: 40 minutes**

NUTRITIONAL ANALYSIS PER SERVING:
Serving Size: 1 burrito

Calories:	190	Cholesterol:	0
Protein:	7 g	Fiber:	5 g
Carbohydrate:	30 g	Sodium:	650 mg
Fat:	5 g	Calcium	48 mg
		Iron	3 mg

Diabetic Exchanges: 2 starches, 1 vegetable

Peanutty Carrot Loaf

*Make vegetable patties from this recipe by adding more bread crumbs
until the desired consistency is reached; cook in a nonstick skillet sprayed
with nonfat cooking spray.*

8-INCH SQUARE BAKING DISH / 6 PORTIONS

1   teaspoon hot sesame oil or olive oil
1   small onion, chopped
4   raw carrots, shredded
2   small zucchini, shredded
⅓   cup dry-roasted, unsalted peanuts
¾   cup breadcrumbs
¼   cup flour
¼   cup nonfat egg substitute
1   teaspoon baking powder
1   Tablespoon parsley
½   teaspoon oregano
½   teaspoon salt
     Dash of pepper
     Nonfat cooking spray

Preheat oven to 350°F. Spray 8-inch square baking dish or 8 x 4-inch loaf
pan with nonfat cooking spray. In a skillet, sauté the onion in the oil for a
minute; remove from heat. Using a food processor or cheese grater, shred
the carrots and zucchini. Chop peanuts in food processor or blender.
Add all of the ingredients to the sautéed onion in the skillet and stir to
blend evenly.

Place in either a prepared 8-inch square baking dish or loaf pan. To make
patties, add bread crumbs if needed, and cook in a prepared skillet.

Bake at 350°F for 25 to 30 minutes, or until the loaf begins to brown
on top. **Prep/bake time: 1 hour**

NUTRITIONAL ANALYSIS PER SERVING:
Serving Size: 1 portion

Calories:	160	Cholesterol:	0
Protein:	7 g	Fiber:	3 g
Carbohydrate:	22 g	Sodium:	320 mg
Fat:	5 g	Calcium	111 mg
		Iron	5 mg

Diabetic Exchanges: 1 starch, 1 protein, 1 vegetable

Soy-Oat Burgers

This basic recipe can be made into a loaf or burgers.
Top these burgers with catsup, barbecue sauce, Mushroom Gravy on page 51,
or a fat-free commercial gravy.

8 X 4-INCH LOAF / 6 SLICES OR 6 BURGERS

1   cup cooked brown rice
½   cup uncooked oatmeal
¾   cup boiling water
1   16-ounce can soybeans, or navy beans,
     rinsed and drained
¼   cup onion, chopped
1   carrot, grated
1   Tablespoon soy sauce
½   teaspoon celery salt
2   Tablespoons fresh parsley, chopped
½   teaspoon garlic powder
¼   teaspoon paprika
¼   cup nonfat egg substitute
½   cup shredded nonfat Cheddar cheese (optional)
     Nonfat cooking spray

Cook rice according to package directions. Pour boiling water over
oatmeal and let set for 10 minutes. Mash soybeans in blender or food
processor. Spray a 2-quart saucepan with cooking spray and sauté the onion.
Remove from heat and add remaining ingredients. Add oatmeal and soybeans. Mix all ingredients together. Add the nonfat cheddar cheese, if
desired. *To make a loaf:* Place mixture in 8 x 4-inch loaf pan sprayed with
cooking spray. Bake 50 to 60 minutes at 350°F. *To make burgers:* Press mixture into 6 patties, adding a little flour if needed for a firmer consistency. Roll
in cornmeal, if desired. Bake at 350°F for 35 minutes or cook in a skillet.
Prep/cook time: 1 hour

NUTRITIONAL ANALYSIS PER SERVING:
Serving Size: 1 burger

Calories:	210	Cholesterol:	0
Protein:	16 g	Fiber:	6 g
Carbohydrate:	22 g	Sodium:	190 mg
Fat:	7 g	Calcium	95 mg
		Iron	5 mg

Diabetic Exchanges: 1 starch, 2 proteins

Chinese Vegetables with Marinated Tofu

This is a variation of the tofu stir-fry. Pea pods or a second pepper can be substituted for the broccoli.

7 1/2 CUPS / 6 PORTIONS

1	pound firm tofu
½	cup water
½	cup light soy sauce
1	teaspoon ground ginger
2	teaspoons olive oil
1	green pepper, sliced
1	carrot, peeled and sliced
1	parsnip, chopped
1	cup broccoli florets
1	cup water
1	Tablespoon soy sauce
2	celery stalks, sliced
2½	cups chopped bok choy (or cabbage)
½	cup mung bean sprouts
1	Tablespoon cornstarch
¼	cup water

Cut tofu in cubes; marinate in mixture of water, soy sauce, and ginger for 20 minutes. Place in an 8-inch square baking dish and bake at 350°F until most of the liquid has been absorbed, about 15 minutes.

In a skillet, sauté the green pepper in the oil. Add remaining ingredients, except the cornstarch and water. Combine cornstarch and ¼ cup water. Pour over vegetable mixture. Stir gently. Add marinated tofu. Simmer until vegetables are just cooked and mixture thickens. Serve over rice, if desired. **Prep/cook time: 35 minutes**

NUTRITIONAL ANALYSIS PER SERVING, WITHOUT RICE:
Serving Size: 1 portion

Calories:	132	Cholesterol:	0
Protein:	10 g	Fiber:	3 g
Carbohydrate:	10 g	Sodium:	800 mg
Fat:	6 g	Calcium	130 mg
		Iron	5 mg

Diabetic Exchanges: 1 protein, 1 vegetable, 1 fat

Mixed Vegetable Curry

This is a good recipe for someone wanting to try tofu for the first time.
It picks up the flavor of the curry nicely.

7 CUPS / 4 SERVINGS

1½ cups rice, uncooked
3   cups water
8   ounces tofu, cubed
1   Tablespoon olive oil
½   teaspoon cumin
1   Tablespoon curry powder, divided
1   onion, sliced
1   cup vegetable broth
3   carrots, sliced
1   green pepper, sliced
½   cup skim milk
1   Tablespoon flour

Measure water in saucepan and heat. Add rice and cook until rice is tender. In a skillet, sauté tofu in the oil; add cumin and 1 teaspoon of the curry. Add the onion and sauté another minute. Add the broth, carrots, green pepper, and remaining curry and simmer until the carrots are done (about 15 to 20 minutes). Turn the heat to low and add the milk. Then sprinkle the flour over the mixture. Continue stirring until mixture thickens. Serve over cooked rice.

Prep/cook time: 40 minutes

NUTRITIONAL ANALYSIS PER SERVING, WITH RICE:
Serving Size: 1¾ cups

Calories:	390	Cholesterol:	0
Protein:	12 g	Fiber:	4 g
Carbohydrate:	69 g	Sodium:	320 mg
Fat:	7 g	Calcium	142 mg
		Iron	7 mg

Diabetic Exchanges: 3 starches, 1 protein, 1 vegetable, 1 fat

Curried Tofu with Sweet Peppers

This recipe is great with homemade Curry (see page 248) or fresh curry powder.

4 CUPS / 4 SERVINGS

8   ounces nonfat plain yogurt
1   Tablespoon fresh curry powder
    or homemade Curry (page 248)
8   ounces firm tofu, cut in small cubes

1   teaspoon oil
1   large onion, sliced
1   clove garlic, crushed
1   green pepper, cut in strips
½   cup vegetable broth
2   Tablespoons slivered almonds (optional)

In a small bowl, blend yogurt and curry together. Cube the tofu and add to the yogurt/curry mixture.

In a skillet, sauté the sliced onion and garlic in the oil. Add the green pepper and the broth as needed to keep vegetable from drying out. Add the yogurt/tofu mixture to the skillet. Stir gently to blend. Cover and cook on low heat for about 15 minutes. Sprinkle almonds on top, if desired. Serve with rice.

Prep/cook time: 50 minutes

NUTRITIONAL ANALYSIS PER SERVING, WITHOUT ALMONDS:
Serving Size: 1 cup

Calories:	280	Cholesterol:	0
Protein:	16 g	Fiber:	1 g
Carbohydrate:	40 g	Sodium:	330 mg
Fat:	6 g	Calcium	249 mg
		Iron	4 mg

Diabetic Exchanges: 1 starch, 2 proteins, 1 vegetable, 1 fat

Sweet and Sour Tofu

If serving over rice or Millet Pilaf on page 161, start the water boiling for the grain first. Pea pods or frozen carrots can be added to this recipe, if you like.

4 CUPS / 4 SERVINGS

Tofu with Broth:
2   cloves garlic, crushed
1   Tablespoon olive oil
8   ounces firm tofu, cubed
1¾ cups water
¼   cup light soy sauce
1   2-inch slice fresh ginger root

Sweet and Sour Sauce:
½   cup broth, from the mixture above
½   cup apple or pineapple juice
2   teaspoons lemon juice
2   Tablespoons apple cider vinegar
¼   cup maple syrup
1½ Tablespoons prepared mustard
2   Tablespoons cornstarch
¼   cup water

Tofu with Broth: In a skillet, sauté the garlic in oil for a minute. Add the cubed tofu, water, soy sauce and ginger root. Bring to a boil, reduce heat, and simmer 15 minutes. Discard ginger root. Remove from the heat and drain ½ cup of this broth into a measuring cup. *Sweet and Sour Sauce:* In a saucepan, combine all sauce ingredients, except the cornstarch and ¼ cup water. Simmer about 10 minutes. Dissolve the cornstarch in the ¼ cup water, add to mixture, and stir until thickened (a few minutes). Pour over tofu mixture in skillet and serve over rice or Millet Pilaf (page 161).
Prep/cook time: 40 minutes

NUTRITIONAL ANALYSIS PER SERVING, WITHOUT RICE:
Serving Size: 1 cup

Calories:	160	Cholesterol:	0
Protein:	6 g	Fiber:	1 g
Carbohydrate:	22 g	Sodium:	450 mg
Fat:	6 g	Calcium	70 mg
		Iron	3 mg

Diabetic Exchanges: 1 starch, 1 protein, 1 fat

Glazed Tofu with Black Bean Sauce

Chinese pea pods, broccoli or carrots can be substituted for the green beans here.
If you use fresh green beans and like them well cooked, steam them first.
The prepared black bean sauce can be found in the supermarket
by other Asian specialty sauces.

6 CUPS / 4 SERVINGS

8	ounces very firm tofu, cut in cubes
2	Tablespoons prepared black bean garlic sauce
1	Tablespoon cornstarch
1	cup rice, uncooked
2	cups water
1	Tablespoon olive oil
1	onion, chopped
1½	cups cut green beans, fresh or frozen
¼	cup white wine
1	Tablespoon soy sauce
2	Tablespoons sugar
½	teaspoon ground ginger
	(or 1 teaspoon fresh grated)
	Dash of red hot pepper sauce (optional)

In a small bowl, combine tofu cubes with black bean sauce and cornstarch. Coat and set aside.

Heat the 2 cups water in a saucepan. Add rice and cook until rice is tender. Add the oil to a hot stir-fry pan and add the tofu cubes. Stir-fry a minute; then add the vegetables and remaining ingredients in the order given. Cook only until the beans are crisp-tender. Serve over rice.

Prep/cook time: 35 minutes

NUTRITIONAL ANALYSIS PER SERVING:
Serving Size: 1½ cups

Calories:	310	Cholesterol:	0
Protein:	10 g	Fiber:	4 g
Carbohydrate:	51 g	Sodium:	290 mg
Fat:	7 g	Calcium	96 mg
		Iron	5 mg

Diabetic Exchanges: 2 starches, 1 protein, 1 vegetable, 1 fat

---

Vegetarian Kabobs with Three Marinades

These kabobs can be either grilled outside or broiled indoors. Since you don't have to worry about killing harmful bacteria with meatless kabobs, just cook them until they're done to your liking. You can use either metal or wooden skewers. If using the wooden ones, soak them in a glass of water for 20 minutes to prevent burning. Precook the potatoes in the microwave.

24 SKEWERS / 6 SERVINGS

Cut any of the following ingredients into chunks:

2	red or green peppers, chunked
1	large onion, chunked
2	cups broccoli florets
1	cup cauliflower, chunked
1	zucchini, chunked
2	potatoes, blanched or precooked in microwave
2	carrots, blanched or precooked in microwave
1	16-ounce container of very firm tofu, cut in chunks
1	Tablespoon olive oil

In a skillet, sauté the tofu chunks in 1 tablespoon of olive oil. Then add all vegetables and tofu to any marinade below and allow to stand at least 30 minutes. Place on skewers and grill until done. If you don't have skewers you can broil on a baking sheet lined with aluminum foil.

(continued on next page)

NUTRITIONAL ANALYSIS PER SERVING:
Serving Size: 4 kabobs of grilled vegetables and 1 Tablespoon each sauce

	4 kabobs	Sweet n' Sour	Curry	Thai-Style
Calories:	135	40	10	20
Protein:	8 g	0	1 g	1 g
Carbohydrate:	17 g	4 g	2 g	2 g
Fat:	4 g	3 g	0	0
Cholesterol:	0	0	0	0
Fiber:	12 g	0	0	0
Sodium:	20 mg	50 mg	60 mg	52 mg
Calcium	115 mg	1 mg	14 mg	2 mg
Iron	3 mg	0	0	0

Diabetic Exchanges: 1 protein, 3 vegetables, 1 fat

Sweet 'n Sour Marinade

¼ cup honey
¼ cup sesame or olive oil
½ cup cider vinegar
¼ cup water
½ teaspoon minced garlic
½ teaspoon salt

Curry Marinade

1 cup nonfat plain yogurt
1 Tablespoon curry powder
2 Tablespoons sugar
1 teaspoon minced onion
½ teaspoon salt
¼ cup water

Thai-Style Peanut Marinade

4 scallions, chopped
2 cloves garlic, crushed
¾ cup vegetable broth
¼ cup peanut butter
1 Tablespoon soy sauce
2 Tablespoons lemon or lime juice
2 Tablespoons brown sugar
¼ teaspoon chili powder
½ teaspoon ground ginger

Method for all marinades: Combine all ingredients in glass jar. Cover and shake well. Use for kabobs or store in refrigerator for up to 2 weeks.

Prep/cook time (including marinating time): 90 minutes

Broccoli-Tofu Quiche

This recipe is a flavorful alternative to the typical quiche which is loaded with fat and cholesterol. Onion can be substituted for the leeks.
Use the kind of mushroom you prefer.

9-INCH PIE / 8 SLICES

Crust:
1   cup whole-wheat flour
1   cup white flour
¼   cup oil
⅓   cup water
⅛   teaspoon salt

Filling:
2   cloves garlic, minced or finely chopped
2   leeks, cleaned and sliced (or 1 onion)
6   ounces fresh sliced mushrooms
1   Tablespoon olive oil
¼   cup white wine
1   teaspoon dried basil
½   teaspoon marjoram
1   cup chopped broccoli florets
2   Tablespoons red wine vinegar
½   Tablespoon cumin or Curry Powder
     (page 248)
½   teaspoon salt
¼   teaspoon pepper
½   Tablespoon prepared mustard
     (preferably Dijon)
1½   pounds soft tofu

Crust: Preheat oven to 350°F. Combine the crust ingredients and press into a 9-inch pie plate. *(continued on next page)*

NUTRITIONAL ANALYSIS PER SERVING:
Serving Size: 1 slice

Calories:	275	Cholesterol:	0
Protein:	12 g	Fiber:	5 g
Carbohydrate:	30 g	Sodium:	210 mg
Fat:	12 g	Calcium	120 mg
		Iron	7 mg

Diabetic Exchanges: 1 starch, 1 protein, 1 vegetable, 1 fat

Bake crust for 8 to 10 minutes in preheated oven.

Filling: In a skillet, sauté the garlic, leeks, and mushrooms in the olive oil. Add a little wine or broth if you need more liquid. Sprinkle with basil and marjoram and set aside. Steam the broccoli in a saucepan until done. Rinse broccoli with cold water and add to vegetable mixture. Add remaining ingredients, except the tofu.

Purée the tofu in a blender. Spoon vegetables onto baked crust; pour the tofu over vegetables and stir gently to blend evenly. Bake at 350°F for 30 minutes or until lightly browned. The quiche should be firm. Cool 5 to 10 minutes, then cut.

Prep/cook time: 1½ hours

Thai-Style Tofu

*Prepare cooked rice, if desired, while making this recipe to save
over-all preparation time. Frozen cut carrots work well in this recipe
and will save chopping time.*

6 CUPS / 4 SERVINGS

1	8-ounce can pineapple chunks
8	ounces firm tofu, cut in small cubes
2	Tablespoons soy sauce
2	Tablespoons sherry or wine
1	Tablespoon canola oil
1	clove garlic, minced in a press
1	onion, chopped in chunks
2	cups sliced carrots
1	sweet green pepper, sliced in strips
1	teaspoon ground ginger
2	Tablespoons sugar
1	Tablespoon cornstarch

Drain the pineapple juice into a measuring cup. Add water to make 1 cup
and pour into a small bowl. Add tofu, soy sauce, and sherry and let stand
about 20 minutes. Meanwhile, cut up and measure all the vegetables. In a
skillet, sauté the garlic and onion in the oil; add the tofu mixture. Heat,
while stirring, for a few minutes. Add remaining ingredients, including
pineapple, and heat until carrots are crisp-tender. Serve with rice.

Prep/cook time: 45 minutes

NUTRITIONAL ANALYSIS PER SERVING, WITHOUT RICE:
Serving Size: 1½ cups

Calories:	193	Cholesterol:	0
Protein:	11 g	Fiber:	3 g
Carbohydrate:	28 g	Sodium:	290 mg
Fat:	6 g	Calcium	149 mg
		Iron	7 mg

Diabetic Exchanges: 2 vegetables, 1 protein, 1 fruit, 1 fat

Tempeh-Vegetable Stew

This stew makes a hearty winter lunch.
Spice it up by adding a teaspoon of ginger, if desired.

5 CUPS / 4 SERVINGS

1	8-ounce package tempeh, cubed
2	onions, chopped
1	clove garlic, minced
1	Tablespoon olive oil
2	cups water
½	cup chopped celery
2	carrots, sliced
2	potatoes, peeled and chopped (or 1½ cups chopped parsnips)
½	cup light soy sauce
2	Tablespoons cornstarch
½	cup water

In a soup pot, sauté tempeh, onions, and garlic in the oil for a few minutes. Add remaining ingredients, except cornstarch and ½ cup water. Cook about 20 minutes or until potatoes are done. Add cornstarch to water; pour over tempeh vegetable mixture until the sauce thickens.

Prep/cook time: 40 minutes

NUTRITIONAL ANALYSIS PER SERVING:
Serving Size: 1¼ cups

Calories:	282	Cholesterol:	0
Protein:	17 g	Fiber:	6 g
Carbohydrate:	36 g	Sodium:	1040 mg
Fat:	7 g	Calcium	106 mg
		Iron	2 mg

Diabetic Exchanges: 2 starches, 2 proteins, 1 vegetable, 1 fat

Tempeh with Noodles

*As with almost any Oriental dish, any preferred vegetable can be used that goes
well with ginger and soy sauce. Broccoli or carrots (precooked al dente)
can be substituted for the water chestnuts.*

9 CUPS / 6 SERVINGS

1	8-ounce package noodles (linguini)
1	8-ounce package tempeh (or firm tofu)
1	Tablespoon olive oil
1	small bunch scallions (5 or 6), thinly sliced
1	8-ounce can water chestnuts
¼	cup roasted peanuts, chopped (or toasted sesame seeds)

Dressing:

2	garlic cloves, minced
1	2-inch section fresh ginger, shredded
2	Tablespoons sesame oil or olive oil
¼	cup light soy sauce
⅛	teaspoon cayenne pepper
2	teaspoons maple syrup

Boil noodles in a large saucepan until done. Rinse, drain and set aside.

Meanwhile, cube the tempeh. In a skillet, sauté tempeh in the oil for
4 to 5 minutes. Remove from heat and add scallions, water chestnuts,
and peanuts.

In a small bowl, mix together the dressing ingredients and add to the
tempeh mixture. Pour over the cooked pasta and serve warm or cold.

Prep/cook time: 30 minutes

NUTRITIONAL ANALYSIS PER SERVING:
Serving Size: 1½ cups

Calories:	331	Cholesterol:	0
Protein:	15 g	Fiber:	3 g
Carbohydrate:	43 g	Sodium:	340 mg
Fat:	12 g	Calcium	51 mg
		Iron	3 mg

Diabetic Exchanges: 2 starches, 1 protein, 1 vegetable, 2 fats

Grilled Tempeh Sandwich

*This recipe calls for grilling in a skillet, but the sauce works well
as a marinade prior to grilling outdoors.*

3 CUPS / 4 SERVINGS

1   8-ounce package tempeh, cut in 1-inch pieces
1   Tablespoon olive oil

Sauce:
1½   cups water
¼   cup soy sauce
1   teaspoon mustard (or ¼ teaspoon
     ground ginger)

In a skillet, sauté the tempeh in the oil for 3 to 5 minutes. Meanwhile, in a small bowl, mix all sauce ingredients and add to the tempeh. Simmer for about 8 to 10 minutes. Remove tempeh from the sauce and cool.

To make sandwiches, use pita bread stuffed with tempeh and other vegetables of your choice (lettuce, tomato, onion, etc). Top with mustard or leftover marinade, which has been thickened with a sprinkle of cornstarch in the skillet.

Prep/cook time: 40 minutes

NUTRITIONAL ANALYSIS PER SERVING, NOT INCLUDING PITA BREAD:
Serving Size: ⅔ cup sandwich filling

Calories:	160	Cholesterol:	0
Protein:	12 g	Fiber:	0
Carbohydrate:	12 g	Sodium:	530 mg
Fat:	7 g	Calcium	58 mg
		Iron	2 mg

Diabetic Exchanges: 1 starch, 1 protein, 1 fat

Filipino Pansit

The tempeh gives this dish a nutty flavor, but you can substitute tofu if you prefer. Tempeh can be purchased at most supermarkets or health food stores.

6 CUPS / 4 SERVINGS

8	ounces tempeh, cut in bite-size cubes
2	Tablespoons light soy sauce
2	teaspoons olive oil, divided
1	teaspoon ginger
2	cups vegetable broth (or 1 bouillon cube in equal amount of water)
8	cloves fresh garlic, minced
1	medium onion, chopped
2	carrots, peeled and cut in julienne strips
3	stalks celery, sliced diagonally
1	package fine rice noodles

Place tempeh in a small bowl; add the soy sauce, 1 teaspoon oil, and ginger. Add a cup of the broth to cover. Marinate the tempeh while you're preparing the vegetables.

Mince the garlic and chop the vegetables. Sauté the onion in a large skillet in 1 teaspoon of oil for about 1 minute. Add the garlic and heat, stirring constantly, for another minute. Add the tempeh mixture to the garlic-onion mixture; stir a minute. Add the carrots, celery, and remaining broth. Stir and simmer 5 to 7 minutes. Rinse the rice noodles in a colander and add to the vegetable mixture; stir well. Continue mixing until noodles are soft, but not soggy (about 10 minutes), adding additional broth if needed.

Prep/cook time: 45 minutes

NUTRITIONAL ANALYSIS PER SERVING:
Serving Size: 1½ cups

Calories:	291	Cholesterol:	0
Protein:	13 g	Fiber:	2 g
Carbohydrate:	49 g	Sodium:	580 mg
Fat:	5 g	Calcium	94 mg
		Iron	2 mg

Diabetic Exchanges: 2 starches, 1 protein, 1 vegetable, 1 fat

Vegetarian Meatloaf

Use this recipe to make a meatloaf sandwich for lunch. The barbecue sauce can either be prepared or homemade on page 50.

8 X 4-INCH LOAF / 6 SLICES

1 cup dry TVP® granules*
1 cup boiling water (or vegetable broth)
1 small or ½ large green pepper
¼ cup grated raw carrot
1 Tablespoon olive oil

1 cup uncooked oatmeal
¼ cup prepared Barbecue Sauce (page 50)
½ cup bread crumbs
¼ cup nonfat egg substitute
1 teaspoon basil
½ teaspoon salt (omit if you're using broth)
1 teaspoon dried minced onions (optional)
Dash of pepper
Nonfat cooking spray

Preheat oven to 350°F. Spray 8 x 4-inch loaf pan with cooking spray. In a mixing bowl, add the TVP® to the boiling water and let stand 15 minutes. Meanwhile, sauté the green pepper in the oil and grate the carrot. If you don't use all of the pepper, you can cut a few strips for garnish on top. Add the TVP® to the vegetables and sauté until soft and a little browned. Add a little water if you need more liquid. Remove from heat and add remaining ingredients. Stir well to blend; spoon into prepared loaf pan. Bake for 40 to 45 minutes at 350°F. Cover with tin foil during the last 15 minutes if the edges brown too quickly. **Prep/cook time: 1½ hours**

* You can substitute any brand of textured soy protein in the ground form. Some brands may be flavored with barbecue seasonings.

NUTRITIONAL ANALYSIS PER SERVING:
Serving Size: 1 slice

Calories:	250	Cholesterol:	0
Protein:	22 g	Fiber:	6 g
Carbohydrate:	32 g	Sodium:	360 mg
Fat:	4 g	Calcium	169 mg
		Iron	5 mg

Diabetic Exchanges: 2 starches, 2 proteins

North-of-the-Border Tacos

This is a good way to try TVP® (textured vegetable protein).
TVP® is concentrated soy protein that has been dried.

6 TACOS / 6 SERVINGS

1	cup dry TVP® granules
1	cup hot water
½	large or 1 small green pepper, chopped
1	small onion, chopped
1	Tablespoon olive oil
2	cups mild or medium taco sauce
1	cup chopped lettuce
1	cup chopped tomato
6	soft flour tortilla shells (large ones)

Mix TVP® granules with hot water in a small bowl and let stand
10 minutes. Meanwhile, chop the green pepper and onion; sauté vegetables with the oil in a skillet for a minute. Add the TVP® and sauté on high another few minutes. Add the taco sauce and simmer for about 15 minutes. While simmering, chop the lettuce and tomato and heat the tortillas to soften them. You can soften tortillas by placing on a cooling rack over the steaming skillet.

To assemble: Place about ½ cup of the TVP® mixture on a tortilla, near the center but closer to the side you're working from. Add a little lettuce and tomato. Take the closer side of the tortilla and start rolling the mixture away from you. Fold up the bottom and finish rolling. Take a piece of tin foil and wrap it around the bottom to make the taco easier to eat with your hands.

Prep/cook time: 45 minutes

NUTRITIONAL ANALYSIS PER SERVING:
Serving Size: 1 large taco

Calories:	290	Cholesterol:	0
Protein:	26 g	Fiber:	8 g
Carbohydrate:	33 g	Sodium:	670 mg
Fat:	6 g	Calcium	170 mg
		Iron	5 mg

Diabetic Exchanges: 2 starches, 2 proteins, 1 vegetable

Stuffed Zucchini

You can use leftover rice for this if you have 1½ cups handy.
Taste and season before stuffing the zucchini. Then add a fresh herb to this—
such as basil, rosemary, or thyme. Also good topped with a little prepared
Marinara Sauce on page 52.

2 STUFFED ZUCCHINI / 4 SERVINGS

½	cup TVP® granules
1½	cups hot water, divided
½	cup dry rice (or 1½ cups cooked)
2	medium zucchini
1	Tablespoon olive oil
1	small onion, chopped
4-5	mushrooms (½ cup chopped)
¼	cup vegetable broth
¼	teaspoon garlic salt
⅛	teaspoon cayenne pepper
¼	teaspoon salt
2	egg whites (or ¼ cup nonfat egg substitute)
	Optional topping: 1 tomato, cut in slices
	or 1 Tablespoon sesame seeds

Combine the TVP® and ½ cup hot water in small bowl; soak for 15 minutes.
If you don't have leftover rice, start the rice cooking in a separate saucepan
using 1 cup water.

Trim ends of zucchini; set zucchini in boiling water for about 5 minutes.
Cut zucchini in half lengthwise. Scoop out pulp, leaving shells intact. Chop
pulp into small pieces, reserving any liquid to add later. You should have
about 1 cup of chopped zucchini pulp. *(continued on next page)*

NUTRITIONAL ANALYSIS PER SERVING:
Serving Size: 1 stuffed zucchini half

Calories:	190	Cholesterol:	0
Protein:	10 g	Fiber:	3 g
Carbohydrate:	26 g	Sodium:	280 mg
Fat:	4 g	Calcium	29 mg
		Iron	2 mg

Diabetic Exchanges: 1 starch, 1 protein, 1 vegetable

In a skillet, sauté onion in the oil for a minute. Add TVP® and mushrooms and sauté for another 4 to 5 minutes. Add broth, spices, and zucchini with liquid. Simmer 10 minutes. Remove from heat and add rice and egg whites. Mix well; stuff the 4 zucchini halves. Top with tomato slices or sesame seeds, if desired. Place in a 13 x 9-inch baking dish and bake for 20 minutes at 350°F. **Prep/cook time: 1 hour**

Hearty Seitan Stew

Seitan is a concentrated form of protein from wheat used as a meat substitute. If you can't find cubed seitan, substitute an 8-ounce package of tempeh.

5 CUPS / 3 SERVINGS

1	Tablespoon olive oil
1	cup onion, chopped
3	cups water
1½	cups seitan, diced
1	cup cubed, raw potatoes (or cubed winter squash)
1	cup carrots, sliced
2	Tablespoons light soy sauce
1	bay leaf
1	teaspoon dried basil (or 2 teaspoons fresh)
1	Tablespoon parsley
1	teaspoon cornstarch
¼	cup water

Saute onion with oil in a large stew pot for a few minutes. Add remaining ingredients, except cornstarch and ¼ cup water. Simmer about 20 minutes, or until potatoes and carrots are almost done. Mix cornstarch with ¼ cup water in measuring cup. Add cornstarch mixture to stew. Stir and simmer until the broth thickens. **Prep/cook time: 1 hour**

NUTRITIONAL ANALYSIS PER SERVING:
Serving Size: 1½ cups

Calories:	270	Cholesterol:	0
Protein:	21 g	Fiber:	4 g
Carbohydrate:	35 g	Sodium:	380 mg
Fat:	5 g	Calcium	84 mg
		Iron	2 mg

Diabetic Exchanges: 2 starches, 2 proteins, 1 vegetable

Pasta with "Tomato-Less" Marinara Sauce

If you're tired of the "same old" spaghetti, try this alternative tomato sauce. The seitan adds protein and a meat-like texture. Seitan can usually be purchased from a health food store in prepared or dry mix form.

4 SERVINGS

6	carrots, peeled and sliced
1	celery stalk, sliced
1½	cups water
1	fresh beet, chopped
1	bay leaf
1	teaspoon dried basil
½	teaspoon oregano
¼	cup chopped fresh parsley
¼	teaspoon salt
	Dash black pepper
2	teaspoons olive oil
1	onion, chopped
3	cloves garlic, minced
1	teaspoon soy sauce
1	cup chopped seitan
8	ounces dry spaghetti (4 cups, cooked)

Place first 5 ingredients in a saucepan and boil for 30 minutes. Remove bay leaf and purée in a blender. Set aside. Blend basil, oregano, fresh parsley, salt and pepper together. Set aside. In a skillet, sauté onion and garlic in oil. Add soy sauce, seitan, and spice blend. Stir well. Add puréed vegetables to seitan mixture and simmer 15 minutes. While sauce is simmering, cook pasta, drain and spoon sauce over the cooked pasta. Serve hot.

Prep/cook time: 1¼ hours

NUTRITIONAL ANALYSIS PER SERVING:
Serving Size: 2 cups

Calories:	380	Cholesterol:	0
Protein:	30 g	Fiber:	10 g
Carbohydrate:	63 g	Sodium:	290 mg
Fat:	2 g	Calcium	70 mg
		Iron	2 mg

Diabetic Exchanges: 2 starches, 1 vegetable, 1 fat

Seitan with Sweet Cherry Sauce

Prepare marinade in advance to shorten preparation time to 30 minutes.
Add frozen carrots or fresh pea pods to the seitan if you wish.

6 CUPS / 4 SERVINGS

Marinade:
1	16-ounce can dark, sweet cherries
2	Tablespoons cider or rice wine vinegar
2	Tablespoons catsup
1	Tablespoon tamari or light soy sauce
½	cup water
2	Tablespoons sugar

6	ounces seitan, cut in thin (¼-inch) strips

1	cup rice, uncooked
2	cups water
1	onion, sliced
2	red or green peppers, sliced
2	teaspoons olive oil

In advance, prepare the marinade by draining the juice from the cherries into a sealable container. Add 6 or 7 cherries to the juice; then add remaining marinade ingredients. Add seitan and store in the refrigerator for at least 30 minutes.

Measure 2 cups water in a saucepan to cook the rice. In a skillet, sauté the onion and green pepper in the oil for a minute. Add the seitan with marinade and simmer for 15 minutes. Serve over the cooked rice.

Prep/cook time: 1 hour, including preparation of marinade

NUTRITIONAL ANALYSIS PER SERVING:
Serving Size: 1½ cups

Calories:	270	Cholesterol:	0
Protein:	17 g	Fiber:	3 g
Carbohydrate:	43 g	Sodium:	240 mg
Fat:	3 g	Calcium:	62 mg
		Iron	3 mg

Diabetic Exchanges: 1 starch, 2 proteins, 1 vegetable, 1 fruit

Chapter 8

Main Dish: Pasta & Grains

Main Dish: Pasta & Grains

Pasta with Vinaigrette Dressing

This recipe travels well for a lunch away from home. Substitute any cooked bean for the kidney beans and celery for the pepper, if so desired.

9 CUPS / 6 SERVINGS

2   hard boiled egg whites, chopped
12   ounces corkscrew pasta
     (multicolored or plain)
½   sweet green pepper, chopped
1   16-ounce can kidney beans,
     rinsed and drained

Dressing:
3   Tablespoons olive oil
⅓   cup red wine vinegar or balsamic vinegar
2   Tablespoons water
1   Tablespoon sugar
1   Tablespoon parsley
½   teaspoon dried basil or thyme
½   teaspoon salt
     Dash of pepper

Hard-boil the eggs; separate the whites from the yolks, reserving the whites. Meanwhile, cook the pasta in another saucepan. Chop the green pepper and drain kidney beans. Set aside.

Combine the dressing ingredients in a small bowl. Rinse and drain the pasta in cold water; place in a large serving bowl. Add the cooked egg whites, green pepper and beans. Stir well. Add the dressing and toss to blend evenly. Chill before serving.

Prep/cook time: 40 minutes

NUTRITIONAL ANALYSIS PER SERVING:
Serving Size: 1½ cups

Calories:	330	Cholesterol:	0
Protein:	14 g	Fiber:	8 g
Carbohydrate:	55 g	Sodium:	220 mg
Fat:	6 g	Calcium	32 mg
		Iron	4 mg

Diabetic Exchanges: 3 starches, 1 protein, 1 fat

Pasta Primavera

*There are many variations of this popular dish—feel free to add or delete
almost any similar vegetable.*

12 CUPS / 6 SERVINGS

1   pound vermicelli or angel hair pasta
    (8 cups cooked)
2   small garlic cloves, crushed
1   small or medium zucchini, diced
3   cups chopped fresh tomatoes (or canned)
4-5 large fresh mushrooms, sliced
6   shallots, diced
1   cup chopped broccoli
½   cup canned chick peas
¼   cup fresh Italian parsley
2   Tablespoons fresh basil
½   teaspoon salt
    Pinch of cayenne pepper (optional)
    Nonfat cooking spray

Cook pasta until al denté (firm to the tooth). While pasta is cooking, coat
a large skillet with cooking spray and add all of the remaining ingredients.
Simmer until broccoli is done, adding a little water if necessary for
moisture. Combine vegetable mixture with the cooked and drained pasta.
Serve hot.

Prep/cook time: 40 minutes

NUTRITIONAL ANALYSIS PER SERVING:
Serving Size: 2 cups

Calories:	330	Cholesterol:	0
Protein:	13 g	Fiber:	5 g
Carbohydrate:	67 g	Sodium:	192 mg
Fat:	1 g	Calcium	35 mg
		Iron	4 mg

Diabetic Exchanges: 4 starches, 1 vegetable

Pasta Primavera with Asparagus

This recipe calls for fresh asparagus. But if it is unavailable or too expensive, fresh broccoli or pea pods will work as well.

7 CUPS / 4 SERVINGS

12	ounces vermicelli or angel hair pasta (6 cups, cooked)
½	cup onion, chopped
1	Tablespoon olive oil
½	cup white wine or vegetable broth
1	pound fresh asparagus
2	carrots, sliced (fresh or frozen)
2	Tablespoons soy sauce
1	teaspoon lime juice
½	teaspoon salt
1	cup nonfat Mozzarella cheese, shredded

Bring a large saucepan of water to boil and cook the pasta. In a large skillet, sauté onion in the oil for a minute. Add remaining ingredients and simmer until asparagus is cooked, adding more liquid if necessary. Add cooked and drained pasta. Spoon onto serving plates and sprinkle with the shredded cheese.

Prep/cook time: 30 minutes

NUTRITIONAL ANALYSIS PER SERVING:
Serving Size: 1¾ cups

Calories:	300	Cholesterol:	0
Protein:	15 g	Fiber:	5 g
Carbohydrate:	51 g	Sodium:	520 mg
Fat:	3 g	Calcium	188 mg
		Iron	3 mg

Diabetic Exchanges: 3 starches, 1 protein, 1 vegetable

Vittorio's Ragu with Rigatoni

Use your preferred vegetables in this recipe.
If you cannot find portobello mushrooms, use any available type.

8 CUPS / 4 SERVINGS

1	Tablespoon olive oil
1	large red onion, sliced
1	carrot, sliced
2	stalks celery, sliced
4	cloves garlic, minced
½	cup white wine or vegetable broth
1	cup tomato juice
1	8-ounce can tomato paste
1	8-ounce can artichoke hearts, sliced
2	big (or 4 small) portobello mushrooms, sliced
2	red bell peppers, chopped
1	Tablespoon fresh thyme
	Dash of pepper
8	ounces uncooked rigatoni (4 cups cooked)

In a large skillet, combine oil, onion, carrot, celery, and garlic. Sauté over low heat, very slowly, to let the vegetables caramelize. Add the wine as needed to avoid burning.

When these vegetables are lightly caramelized, add remaining ingredients and simmer on low heat for 20 minutes. While vegetables are simmering, cook pasta in a large saucepan. Drain pasta when al denté (firm to the tooth) and add to the sautéed vegetables. Mix well and serve.

Prep/cook time: 1 hour

NUTRITIONAL ANALYSIS PER SERVING:
Serving Size: 2 cups

Calories:	360	Cholesterol:	0
Protein:	14 g	Fiber:	9 g
Carbohydrate:	65 g	Sodium:	480 mg
Fat:	5 g	Calcium	59 mg
		Iron	6 mg

Diabetic Exchanges: 2 starches, 1 protein, 3 vegetables

Ziti with Fresh Spinach

I highly recommend that you use a fresh broth for this sauce; please refer to the Homemade Vegetable Broth on page 65.

8 CUPS / 4 SERVINGS

12	ounces uncooked ziti (6 cups cooked)
2	large or 3 small cloves garlic, minced
2	teaspoons olive oil
1½	cups Homemade Vegetable Broth (page 65)
3	cups fresh spinach, washed and chopped
1	Tablespoon flour
2	teaspoons lemon juice
½	teaspoon thyme
½	teaspoon salt
	Dash of pepper

Put water on to boil for the ziti and cook separately.

In a skillet, sauté garlic in the hot oil for a minute. Add broth and spinach. While the spinach is cooking, thicken the broth by sprinkling flour over the mixture and stirring well to avoid clumping. Add remaining ingredients, stirring to thicken. Add the cooked and drained pasta; serve immediately.

Prep/cook time: 30 minutes

NUTRITIONAL ANALYSIS PER SERVING:
Serving Size: 2 cups

Calories:	360	Cholesterol:	0
Protein:	13 g	Fiber:	4 g
Carbohydrate:	68 g	Sodium:	450 mg
Fat:	4 g	Calcium	29 mg
		Iron	3 mg

Diabetic Exchanges: 4 starches, 1 vegetable

Raman Noodles with Japanese Sauce

*I've found fresh raman noodles in the supermarket near the tofu
and Asian vegetables. If you can't find them, use fettuccini. While you're in the
Asian vegetable section, you may want to buy fresh gingeroot.*

6 CUPS / 6 SERVINGS

12 ounces fresh raman noodles

Sauce:
2 Tablespoons ginger oil or sesame oil
1 Tablespoon sugar
1 Tablespoon lemon juice
2 Tablespoons light soy sauce
½-1 teaspoon freshly grated ginger (or ground)
2 Tablespoons scallions, chopped
   Dash of pepper
2 Tablespoons sesame seeds

Cook and drain the noodles. Combine sauce ingredients together and mix
well. Pour over cooked and drained noodles. Sprinkle with sesame seeds.
Serve cold.

Prep/cook time: 25 minutes

NUTRITIONAL ANALYSIS PER SERVING:
Serving Size: 1 cup

Calories:	170	Cholesterol:	0
Protein:	5 g	Fiber:	2 g
Carbohydrate:	23 g	Sodium:	270 mg
Fat:	6 g	Calcium	16 mg
		Iron	3 mg

Diabetic Exchanges: 1 starch, 1 fat

Cold Ginger Scallion Noodles

Here is a spicier version of the cold noodle salad. You may want to start with a tiny pinch of hot pepper, then try it and add more to taste. If you're using this for a main dish, add cubed tofu; stir-fry separately and add to the sauté mixture.

8 CUPS / 8 SERVINGS

1	pound capellini or angel hair pasta (8 cups cooked)
1	Tablespoon peanut oil
2	Tablespoons fresh ginger, minced or grated
½	red onion, diced
3	cloves garlic, minced
1	bunch scallions (4 or 5)
¼	cup light soy sauce
¼	cup water
	Pinch of dried hot pepper flakes
1	Tablespoon fresh cilantro
	A steamed vegetable, such as broccoli or carrot sticks (optional)

Cook the angel hair pasta to al denté (firm to the tooth). While pasta is cooking, prepare ginger, onion, garlic, and scallions. Drain pasta, rinse with cold water, and set aside.

In a skillet, sauté the ginger, onion, garlic, and scallions in the oil. Be careful not to burn the garlic or the oil—1 to 2 minutes is plenty. Add the remaining ingredients and cook another 2 minutes. Pour over cold pasta and toss.

Prep/cook time: 30 minutes

NUTRITIONAL ANALYSIS PER SERVING:			
Serving Size: 1 cup			
Calories:	240	Cholesterol:	0
Protein:	9 g	Fiber:	3 g
Carbohydrate:	44 g	Sodium:	260 mg
Fat:	2 g	Calcium	24 mg
		Iron	2 mg
Diabetic Exchanges: 3 starches			

Fettuccini with Broccoli Casserole

A great pasta and broccoli combo; this could be prepared in advance
for a potluck supper.

9 X 13-INCH BAKING DISH / 9 PORTIONS

1	small onion, chopped
7-8	fresh mushrooms, sliced
2	cups chopped fresh broccoli florets
1	Tablespoon olive oil
½	cup white wine
12	ounces uncooked fettuccini (or similar pasta, 6 cups cooked)
2	cups 1% lowfat cottage cheese
1	cup skim milk
½	cup nonfat egg substitute
½	teaspoon dried rosemary
¼	cup seasoned bread crumbs
½	cup shredded nonfat Cheddar cheese
	Nonfat cooking spray

Preheat oven to 350°F. Spray 9 x 13-inch baking dish with cooking spray. In a large skillet, sauté the first 3 ingredients in olive oil for a minute. Add the wine and simmer until broccoli is crisp-tender. Meanwhile, add pasta to boiling water and cook until al dente.

Remove skillet from heat and add the cottage cheese, milk, egg substitute and rosemary. Mix well. Drain and rinse the pasta; blend with the vegetables.

Spread mixture in a 9 x 13-inch baking dish. Sprinkle with bread crumbs and shredded cheese. Bake for 45 minutes at 350°F. Cover baking dish with tin foil for first 30 minutes. **Prep/bake time: 1¼ hours**

NUTRITIONAL ANALYSIS PER SERVING:
Serving Size: 1 portion

Calories:	260	Cholesterol:	5 mg
Protein:	18 g	Fiber:	2 g
Carbohydrate:	36 g	Sodium:	360 mg
Fat:	3 g	Calcium	148 mg
		Iron	3 mg

Diabetic Exchanges: 2 starches, 1 protein, 1 vegetable

Zucchini Lasagna

Traditional lasagna is prohibitively high in fat. Here is a recipe that allows you to enjoy this popular dish while adhering to a lowfat dietary plan.

9 X 13-INCH BAKING DISH / 12 SERVINGS

1	medium onion, chopped
1	clove garlic, minced
1	Tablespoon olive oil
1½	cups chopped zucchini
1	cup sliced fresh mushrooms
1	teaspoon dried basil
½	teaspoon dried oregano
16	ounces (2 cups) skim milk ricotta cheese
2	tablespoons fresh parsley
2	egg whites
2	26-ounce jars tomato or pasta sauce, divided
1	16-ounce package lasagna noodles
2	cups shredded lowfat Mozzarella cheese, divided

In a saucepan, sauté onion and garlic in oil. Add zucchini, mushrooms, basil and oregano. Then add 2 cups of the tomato sauce. Simmer 5 to 10 minutes. Meanwhile, combine ricotta cheese with the parsley and egg whites. Set aside. Cook lasagna noodles until almost fully cooked; drain and immerse in cold water. Drain again. To assemble, pour some of the tomato sauce onto the bottom of a 9 x 13-inch baking dish. Lay a flat layer of 4 lasagna noodles, then ½ of the vegetable mixture. Sprinkle with 1 cup of the Mozzarella cheese. Repeat a layer of 4 lasagna noodles, then top with the ricotta mixture. Add the third layer of noodles, the remaining vegetable mixture, and the remaining Mozzarella cheese. Top with more tomato sauce. Bake at 350°F for 45 minutes or until sauce bubbles.

Prep/bake time: 1¾ hours

NUTRITIONAL ANALYSIS PER SERVING:
Serving Size: 1 portion

Calories:	250	Cholesterol:	5 mg
Protein:	17 g	Fiber:	3 g
Carbohydrate:	36 g	Sodium:	620 mg
Fat:	4 g	Calcium	219 mg
		Iron	2 mg

Diabetic Exchanges: 2 starches, 1 protein, 1 vegetable

Quick and Easy Broccoli Casserole

*One of my patients frequently makes this lasagna-like casserole
because it's simple and filling.*

8-INCH SQUARE BAKING DISH / 6 PORTIONS

6 ounces uncooked elbow macaroni
(3 cups cooked)
3 cups fresh broccoli, chopped
2 cups nonfat cottage cheese
2 Tablespoons dried parsley
¼ cup nonfat egg substitute
1 28-ounce jar spaghetti sauce

In a saucepan, cook chopped broccoli until done. Meanwhile, put a pot of
water on to cook the macaroni. In a blender, add the cottage cheese,
parsley and egg substitute. When the broccoli has cooked and cooled a bit,
add half of the broccoli and blend. Add the remaining broccoli and
blend again.

Preheat oven to 350°F. Cook and drain the macaroni. Layer in an 8-inch
square baking dish the following: ¼ of the spaghetti sauce, ½ of the macaroni, ½ of the broccoli-cheese mixture. Repeat the layers. Then top with
sauce. (You may only need about 20 ounces of the sauce.)
Bake 25 minutes at 350°F.

Prep/bake time: 1 hour

NUTRITIONAL ANALYSIS PER SERVING:
Serving Size: 1 portion

Calories:	250	Cholesterol:	5 mg
Protein:	16 g	Fiber:	3 g
Carbohydrate:	33 g	Sodium:	490 mg
Fat:	3 g	Calcium	83 mg
		Iron	2 mg

Diabetic Exchanges: 2 starches, 1 protein, 1 vegetable

Spicy Eggplant Pasta

This is good served either hot or cold. The red pepper is spicy; so you can vary the amount according to your taste. If you use salted canned tomatoes, you may want to omit added salt.

9 CUPS / 6 SERVINGS

12	ounces rigatoni, or similar pasta (6 cups cooked)
1	small eggplant, peeled and cubed*
2	Tablespoons olive oil
2	cloves fresh garlic, minced
2	cups chopped fresh tomatoes (or canned)
1	teaspoon crushed red pepper
½	teaspoon salt
¼	cup fresh parsley
¼	cup chopped scallion (or onion, if you prefer)

Put water on to boil for the pasta and begin chopping the vegetables. Steam the eggplant separately, until soft. Cook and drain the pasta.

In a large saucepan, sauté the garlic in the oil and add remaining ingredients. Toss all ingredients together and heat thoroughly.

*You can leave the skin on the eggplant if you like. But some skins are a little bitter; it may be best to peel it. Slice the eggplant first; then lightly salt and press by placing a plate over slices in the sink. Let the juices drain while you prepare the water for the pasta and prepare tomatoes and garlic. Then rinse the eggplant slices in water before chopping.

Prep/cook time: 1 hour

NUTRITIONAL ANALYSIS PER SERVING:
Serving Size: 1½ cups

Calories:	270	Cholesterol:	0
Protein:	9 g	Fiber:	5 g
Carbohydrate:	48 g	Sodium:	190 mg
Fat:	6 g	Calcium	18 mg
		Iron	3 mg

Diabetic Exchanges: 2 starches, 1 vegetable, 1 fat

Basic Risotto

The northern Italians cook a rice that is a plump, moist variation of our boiled rice. It requires frequent stirring, but the cooking time is shorter.

3 CUPS / 4 SERVINGS

½   small onion, chopped
1   Tablespoon olive oil
1   cup arborio or short grain rice, uncooked
1   cup vegetable broth
1½ cups warm water

In a large saucepan, sauté the onion in the oil. Add the uncooked rice and cook for a few minutes. Combine vegetable broth and warm water together in a large measuring cup. Add 1 cup of the liquid to the rice and bring to a boil. Keep on low boil, stirring frequently, for 15 minutes, adding the remainder of liquid when first cup gets absorbed. Do not cover. Rice is done when the grain is fully cooked but still moist.

Prep/cook time: 35 minutes

NUTRITIONAL ANALYSIS PER SERVING:
Serving Size: ¾ cup

Calories:	210	Cholesterol:	0
Protein:	4 g	Fiber:	1 g
Carbohydrate:	39 g	Sodium:	190 mg
Fat:	4 g	Calcium	16 mg
		Iron	2 mg

Diabetic Exchanges: 2 starches

Spinach-Rice Medley

Broccoli can be substituted for the spinach and a bouillon cube dissolved in a little hot water can be substituted for the granules. This would complement a veggie-burger or a tofu dish.

4 CUPS / 4 SERVINGS

1	10-ounce package frozen chopped spinach, thawed
1	teaspoon olive oil
½	cup sweet red pepper, chopped
½	cup onion, chopped
¼	cup nonfat egg substitute
⅓	cup skim milk
1	teaspoon vegetable bouillon granules
¼	teaspoon pepper
1	cup cooked rice
	Nonfat cooking spray

Preheat oven to 350°F. Coat 1½-quart casserole dish with nonfat cooking spray. Thaw and drain spinach. In a skillet, sauté onion and red pepper in the oil until tender. Remove from heat and add remaining ingredients. Spoon into prepared casserole dish.

Bake for 25 to 30 minutes at 350°F.

Prep/cook time: 45 minutes

NUTRITIONAL ANALYSIS PER SERVING:
Serving Size: 1 cup

Calories:	120	Cholesterol:	0
Protein:	7 g	Fiber:	3 g
Carbohydrate:	21 g	Sodium:	370 mg
Fat:	1 g	Calcium	116 mg
		Iron	3 mg

Diabetic Exchanges: 1 starch, 1 vegetable

Rice Pilaf-Indian Style

Use a large skillet with a cover for this one-dish meal.
It has a terrific aroma while cooking.

5 CUPS / 4 SERVINGS

1	small onion, chopped
½	of green pepper
1	Tablespoon sesame or olive oil
2	cups water
1	cup frozen (or fresh) cut-up green beans
½	cup frozen corn
1	cup rice (basmati or enriched white), uncooked
½	teaspoon salt
1	teaspoon curry powder
½	teaspoon cumin
¼	teaspoon cinnamon
¼	teaspoon nutmeg
1	large bay leaf
¼	cup dry roasted cashews

In a large skillet, sauté the onion and green pepper in the oil for a minute or two. Add the water, beans and corn. Heat to boiling, then reduce heat and add the rice and spices. Cover and simmer 20 to 25 minutes, until the water is absorbed. Check after 15 minutes to make sure the rice doesn't dry out. Add cashews and serve.

Prep/cook time: 45 minutes

NUTRITIONAL ANALYSIS PER SERVING:
Serving Size: 1¼ cups

Calories:	270	Cholesterol:	0
Protein:	6 g	Fiber:	3 g
Carbohydrate:	50 g	Sodium:	300 mg
Fat:	5 g	Calcium	147 mg
		Iron	3 mg

Diabetic Exchanges: 2 starches, 1 protein, 1 vegetable

"Stir-Fried" Rice Delux

This is a quick and satisfying skillet meal. Fresh bean sprouts, broccoli, or water chestnuts can be substituted for the vegetables.

4 1/2 CUPS / 3 SERVINGS

1	medium onion, sliced
¾	cup nonfat vegetable broth (or white wine)
2	teaspoons ground ginger
1	clove garlic, crushed
1	cup sliced carrots, fresh or frozen
1	cup pea pods, with ends trimmed
2½	cups cooked rice
2	Tablespoons light soy sauce
4	egg whites, slightly beaten with a fork
1	teaspoon olive oil
	Nonfat cooking spray

Spray a large skillet with cooking spray and sauté the onion for a minute. Add the broth, ginger, garlic and vegetables. Cook over medium heat for about 10 minutes. Add the rice and soy sauce. If using fresh carrots, add a little more water and heating time if necessary.

In a small skillet, heat olive oil on medium heat. Add egg whites and cook until they turn solid white. Chop with a spatula or large spoon until the whites are in small cooked pieces. Add to rice mixture and serve immediately.

Prep/cook time: 30 minutes

NUTRITIONAL ANALYSIS PER SERVING:
Serving Size: 1½ cups

Calories:	280	Cholesterol:	0
Protein:	12 g	Fiber:	4 g
Carbohydrate:	52 g	Sodium:	430 mg
Fat:	2 g	Calcium	60
		Iron	3 mg

Diabetic Exchanges: 2 starches, 1 protein, 2 vegetables

Millet Patties

Millet can be found at any health food store and most supermarkets.

6 PATTIES

1 cup uncooked millet
4 cups water
1 vegetable bouillon cube

1 carrot, grated
2 scallions, chopped
¼ cup fresh chopped parsley
½ teaspoon garlic powder
2 teaspoons tamari or light soy sauce
½ teaspoon salt
   Dash of cayenne pepper
½ cup bread crumbs
2 Tablespoons canola oil for cooking
   Corn meal for coating patties
   Nonfat cooking spray

Preparation of millet: Spray a saucepan with cooking spray. Over medium heat, toast the millet for a minute or two, stirring constantly. Add water and bouillon cube. Bring to a boil and stir. Cover, reduce heat, and simmer for 35 minutes. Let set 10 minutes off the heat before removing lid. Cool.

Meanwhile, combine vegetables, spices, soy sauce, and bread crumbs in a mixing bowl. Add the cooled millet. Add more bread crumbs, if necessary, to get the consistency for patties. Shape into 6 patties and roll in corn meal. You may freeze some at this stage for a quick meal later. In a skillet, heat oil and cook patties until brown and crispy. If you prefer, you can bake these for 20 to 25 minutes in a 350°F oven. Serve with Mushroom Gravy (page 51) or tomato sauce. **Prep/cook time: 1½ hours**

NUTRITIONAL ANALYSIS PER SERVING:
Serving Size: 1 patty

Calories:	120	Cholesterol:	0
Protein:	3 g	Fiber:	1 g
Carbohydrate:	21 g	Sodium:	280 mg
Fat:	3 g	Calcium	24 mg
		Iron	1 mg

Diabetic Exchanges: 1 starch, 1 vegetable

Millet Pilaf

This goes well with Sweet and Sour Tofu on page 126.

4 CUPS / 6 SERVINGS

2½ cups millet, uncooked
1   Tablespoon safflower or canola oil
1   medium onion, chopped
1   large carrot, diced or shredded
1   red pepper, cut in strips
3½ cups water
½   teaspoon salt
    Pepper to taste

Wash and drain millet. Set aside. In a large saucepan, sauté the onion, carrot, and pepper in the oil for 2 minutes. Add millet and sauté another 5 to 7 minutes. If necessary, add a little of the measured water to prevent burning. Add the water and bring to a boil. Reduce heat, cover, and simmer 30 minutes. Season with salt and pepper.

Prep/cook time: 50 minutes

NUTRITIONAL ANALYSIS PER SERVING:
Serving Size: ⅔ cup

Calories:	110	Cholesterol:	0
Protein:	4 g	Fiber:	2 g
Carbohydrate:	20 g	Sodium:	180 mg
Fat:	2 g	Calcium	11 mg
		Iron	1 mg

Diabetic Exchanges: 1 starch, 1 vegetable

Grilled Polenta with Mushroom Sauce

Make your own polenta, see Polenta di Palermo on page 164
or use the box mix to make this recipe.

9 X 13-INCH BAKING DISH / 8 PORTIONS

½   package instant polenta
2   teaspoons olive oil
¼   cup diced onion
3   cloves garlic, minced
2   shallots, minced
3   cups sliced fresh mushrooms
¼   cup dried porcini mushrooms, soaked
    in 2 cups hot water
¼   cup dry sherry or wine (optional)
4   sprigs fresh thyme
½   teaspoon salt
    Pepper to taste
½   cup shredded lowfat Cheddar cheese
    (optional)
    Nonfat cooking spray

Coat a 9 x 13-inch baking dish with cooking spray.

Cook polenta according to package directions. Spread on prepared baking dish so that the polenta will be ½-inch thick. Refrigerate polenta until it is solid enough to cut into squares. Cut 4 squares, then cut diagonally to make 8 triangles.

Heat a skillet or broiler; spray with cooking spray. Carefully remove triangles with a spatula and add to skillet. Grill or broil on both sides until slightly brown.

(continued on next page)

NUTRITIONAL ANALYSIS PER SERVING:
Serving Size: 1 portion polenta with ⅔ cup sauce

Calories:	210	Cholesterol:	0
Protein:	6 g	Fiber:	2 g
Carbohydrate:	42 g	Sodium:	140 mg
Fat:	3 g	Calcium	5 mg
		Iron	1 mg

Diabetic Exchanges: 2 starches, 1 vegetable

While polenta is cooking, heat olive oil in a saucepan. Sauté onion, garlic and shallots in the oil. Add sliced mushrooms, porcini mushrooms, and about 1 cup of the porcini liquid. Cook until mushrooms are soft. Add sherry, thyme, salt, and pepper. Reduce to a sauce consistency; if necessary, sprinkle with a pinch of flour to thicken.

Place polenta triangle on a plate and top with mushroom sauce. Sprinkle with a little shredded lowfat cheese, if desired.

Prep/cook time: 50 minutes

Polenta di Palermo

Making polenta is a little tricky; you need to stir it until you think it is done,
then probably stir another minute more. As it cools,
it should be solid enough to cut through.

16-INCH SQUARE OF POLENTA WITH 4 CUPS
SAUCE / 4 SERVINGS

Polenta:
3   cups water
¾   cup yellow cornmeal
½   teaspoon salt
1   Tablespoon olive oil
1   teaspoon fresh basil (or ½ teaspoon dried)
1   teaspoon oil for the pan

Sauce:
1   medium onion, chopped
1   green pepper, chopped
1   teaspoon olive oil
1   16-ounce can chick peas, drained
1   28-ounce can peeled tomatoes
½   teaspoon dried basil
½   teaspoon dried oregano

Polenta: Measure water in a large saucepan; add the salt. Bring the water
to a simmer. Slowly whisk in the cornmeal to avoid lumps. Add the olive
oil and basil while constantly stirring over heat high enough to make the
polenta bubble slowly. In about 10 to 15 minutes it should thicken to a muffin batter consistency. Stir another minute; when mixture is stiff and pulls
away from the side of the pan, place on an oiled baking sheet. Form a 16 x
16-inch square and set aside. *(continued on next page)*

NUTRITIONAL ANALYSIS PER SERVING:
Serving Size: 4 x 4-inch polenta square with 1 cup sauce

Calories:	290	Cholesterol:	0
Protein:	10 g	Fiber:	9 g
Carbohydrate:	47 g	Sodium:	300 mg
Fat:	7 g	Calcium	20 mg
		Iron	1 mg

Diabetic Exchanges: 2 starches, 1 protein, 1 vegetable, 1 fat

Sauce: In a skillet, sauté the onion and pepper in the oil. Add the remaining ingredients and simmer 15 to 20 minutes. While the sauce is simmering, cut 4 squares in the polenta. With a spatula, carefully move each square onto a serving plate (polenta still may be a little mushy). Serve sauce over squares of polenta.

Prep/cook time: 45 minutes

Chapter 9

Vegetables:
Main Dish & On-the-Side

Vegetables: Main Dish & On-the-Side

Ratatouille

Here's a one-pot meal that can be reheated in the microwave for leftovers.

6 CUPS / 4 SERVINGS

1	Tablespoon olive oil
1	medium onion, chopped
1	sweet red pepper, sliced in strips
1	small zucchini, sliced
1	small eggplant, peeled and chopped
2	cups chopped fresh tomatoes (or canned, crushed tomatoes)
1	15-ounce can cannellini beans, rinsed and drained
1	Tablespoon dried basil
1	Tablespoon dried parsley
1	teaspoon marjoram
½	teaspoon salt
	Pepper to taste
¼	cup white wine, as needed
½	cup shredded nonfat Mozzarella cheese

In a large soup pot, sauté onion and red pepper in oil. Add remaining ingredients, except the cheese, and cook over medium heat until vegetables are tender (20 minutes). Add white wine if you need more liquid. Serve in bowls, topped with the shredded cheese.

Prep/cook time: 50 minutes

NUTRITIONAL ANALYSIS PER SERVING:
Serving Size: 1½ cups

Calories:	190	Cholesterol:	0
Protein:	14 g	Fiber:	7 g
Carbohydrate:	24 g	Sodium:	540 mg
Fat:	4 g	Calcium	285 mg
		Iron	2 mg

Diabetic Exchanges: 1 protein, 2 vegetables

Stuffed Squash

*This makes a substantial lunch, but you may want to add
a soup or salad for dinner.*

4 SERVINGS

2   butternut squash
1   Tablespoon olive oil
1   cup chopped fresh mushrooms
1   small onion, chopped
2-3 Tablespoons white wine
1   6-ounce box long grain and wild rice mix
2   Tablespoons chopped walnuts or peanuts
2   egg whites

Preheat oven to 350°F. Split the 2 butternut squash lengthwise and remove seeds. Bake, face down for about 35 minutes at 350°F.

Meanwhile, sauté mushrooms and onion in the oil. Add wine for moisture. Cook the wild rice mix according to package directions. Remove vegetables from the heat; add the cooked rice. When this mixture has cooled a bit, add nuts and egg whites. Fill the 4 cavities of the cooked squash and bake another 25 minutes at 350°F.

Prep/cook time: 1¼ hours

NUTRITIONAL ANALYSIS PER SERVING:
Serving Size: ½ squash

Calories:	270	Cholesterol:	0
Protein:	10 g	Fiber:	8 g
Carbohydrate:	45 g	Sodium:	650 mg
Fat:	6 g	Calcium	75 mg
		Iron	1 mg

Diabetic Exchanges: 2 starches, 1 protein, 1 vegetable

Veggie-Pita Sandwiches

If packing for lunch away from home, take dressing separately and add it just before eating. Add fresh fruit, if desired, as this is very low in calories.

2 PITA POCKETS / 2 SERVINGS

1	large whole wheat pita bread, cut in half
6	slices cucumber
¼	cup diced green pepper (or celery)
½	cup alfalfa sprouts
1	medium tomato, chopped
½	cup shredded nonfat Cheddar cheese
2	Tablespoons light Italian dressing

In a small bowl, combine cucumber, green pepper, alfalfa sprouts, tomato, and cheese. Stuff vegetable-cheese mixture into the two pita halves. Drizzle each sandwich with a tablespoon of dressing.

Variations: Add 2 hard-boiled egg whites, a shredded carrot or spinach leaves to line pita pockets.

Prep/cook time: 15 minutes

NUTRITIONAL ANALYSIS PER SERVING:
Serving Size: 1 pita half

Calories:	140	Cholesterol:	0
Protein:	12 g	Fiber:	4 g
Carbohydrate:	21 g	Sodium:	640 mg
Fat:	1 g	Calcium	258 mg
		Iron	1 mg

Diabetic Exchanges: 1 starch, 1 vegetable

Spinach and Cheese Wontons

*Fold these by hand or use a calzone/pastry press available in kitchen
appliance stores.*

8 WONTONS / 4 SERVINGS

1   10-ounce bag fresh spinach
1   cup part-skim ricotta cheese
1   apple, peeled and chopped
½   cup nonfat egg substitute
½   teaspoon cumin
½   teaspoon salt
8   egg roll wrappers
    Nonfat cooking spray

Wilt spinach by steaming or boiling in a small amount of water. Drain and chop roughly. Place in a mixing bowl; add remaining ingredients, leaving a tablespoon of egg substitute in the carton to brush on the wonton later.

Place each wonton wrapper on a cutting board or in the pastry press. Add about 2 tablespoons of filling in the center and fold over to make a triangle or press in the press. Secure edges with a wet fork, cut off extra wonton skin and brush the top with a little remaining egg substitute.

Place on a shallow baking dish that has been sprayed with cooking spray. Bake at 350°F for 20 minutes, or until edges are brown and crispy.

Prep/bake time: 45 minutes

NUTRITIONAL ANALYSIS PER SERVING:
Serving Size: 2 wontons

Calories:	190	Cholesterol:	20 mg
Protein:	14 g	Fiber:	3 g
Carbohydrate:	20 g	Sodium:	550 mg
Fat:	7 g	Calcium	263 mg
		Iron	3 mg

Diabetic Exchanges: 1 starch, 1 protein, 1 vegetable, 1 fat

Easy Eggplant Casserole

Here's a tasty lowfat version of an Italian favorite. Use the lowfat versus the non-fat cheese because it makes a difference in the flavor of this dish.

9-INCH SQUARE BAKING DISH / 6 PORTIONS

2	small or 1 large eggplant, peeled
¼	cup nonfat egg substitute
2	Tablespoons water
⅔	cup dried bread crumbs (Italian or plain)
1	8-ounce can tomato sauce
½	teaspoon oregano
1	teaspoon fresh or ½ teaspoon dried basil
1	8-ounce package sliced lowfat Mozzarella cheese Nonfat cooking spray

Preheat oven to 350°F. Spray cookie sheet and 9-inch square baking dish with cooking spray. Cut peeled eggplant into ½ inch thick slices. Mix egg substitute with water. Dip eggplant slices into the egg mixture; then coat with bread crumbs. Lay coated eggplant slices onto a cookie sheet sprayed with cooking spray. Bake at 350°F for about 15 minutes or until brown on one side; then turn and brown on the other side.

In a small bowl, add oregano and basil to tomato sauce. In prepared 9-inch square baking dish, layer ½ of the eggplant slices, ½ of the seasoned tomato sauce, then ½ of the cheese. Repeat the layers. Bake for about 30 minutes at 350°F.

Hint: You can prepare the eggplant slices either 1 hour before serving or the day before and store refrigerated. Leftover eggplant can be placed in pita bread for easy-to-carry eggplant sandwiches.

Prep/bake time: 1 hour

NUTRITIONAL ANALYSIS PER SERVING:
Serving Size: 1 portion

Calories:	210	Cholesterol:	20 mg
Protein:	15 g	Fiber:	5 g
Carbohydrate:	21 g	Sodium:	550 mg
Fat:	8 g	Calcium	320 mg
		Iron	2 mg

Diabetic Exchanges: 1 starch, 2 proteins, 1 vegetable

Basic Homemade Pizza

Don't hesitate to make two pizzas—they freeze well. If you prefer, you can freeze one half of the dough after you punch it down and divide in half.

2 12-INCH PIZZAS

Crust:

1	package yeast
1	Tablespoon sugar
1	cup warm water
3	cups all-purpose flour
2	teaspoons salt
1	teaspoon olive oil
	Nonfat cooking spray
1	Tablespoon cornmeal

Toppings:

½	cup shredded lowfat Mozzarella cheese
½	green bell pepper, chopped
1	small onion, sliced
2-3	fresh mushrooms, sliced
	Chopped tomatoes or tomato sauce
	Oregano, parsley, basil
	Crushed garlic

Dissolve yeast and sugar in water and let stand in a large bowl for 5 minutes. Stir in 2¾ cups flour, salt, and oil. Form a soft dough; then knead on a floured board until smooth and elastic (5 minutes) while adding remaining flour. Place dough in a bowl coated with cooking spray. Then turn to coat top. Cover and let rise in a warm place (about 1 hour). Punch dough down and divide in half.

Spray 2 pizza pans or 2 cookie sheets with cooking spray and dust with cornmeal. *(continued on next page)*

NUTRITIONAL ANALYSIS PER SERVING:
Serving Size: ⅛ of a 12-inch pizza

Calories:	290	Cholesterol:	10 mg
Protein:	11 g	Fiber:	2 g
Carbohydrate:	52 g	Sodium:	800 mg
Fat:	4 g	Calcium	133 mg
		Iron	3 mg

Diabetic Exchanges: 2 starches, 1 protein, 2 vegetables

Roll dough into 12-inch circles or rectangles. Crimp edges of dough to form a rim. Cover and let rise for 30 minutes. Top with toppings and bake at 475°F for 10 to 15 minutes, or until crust is golden brown.

Prep/cook time: 2½ hours

Pizza with Sautéed Mushrooms

This recipe calls for making the dough in a bread machine. If you don't have a machine, knead the dough manually as you would for bread. Sweet peppers or eggplant can be substituted for the mushrooms, if you prefer.

1 12-INCH PIZZA / 4 SERVINGS

Crust:

1	cup warm water
3	cups unbleached all-purpose or bread flour
1	Tablespoon sugar
½	teaspoon salt
1	teaspoon yeast

Toppings:

1	medium onion, sliced
4-5	fresh mushrooms, sliced
2	teaspoons olive oil
⅔	cup peeled, crushed tomatoes
½	teaspoon basil
¼	teaspoon oregano
¾	cup light Laughing Cow® cheese (or a soft lowfat cheese)
1	Tablespoon cornmeal

Crust: Place all ingredients in bread machine in the order given. Start and run the machine until the first punch down time *(continued on next page)*

NUTRITIONAL ANALYSIS PER SERVING:
Serving Size: ¼ of 12-inch pizza

Calories:	429	Cholesterol:	5 mg
Protein:	12 g	Fiber:	5 g
Carbohydrate:	84 g	Sodium:	420 mg
Fat:	4 g	Calcium	59 mg
		Iron	3 mg

Diabetic Exchanges: 4 starches, 1 protein, 2 vegetables

(usually 45 or 50 minutes). Meanwhile, prepare the toppings.

Toppings: Slice the onion and mushrooms. In a skillet, sauté in the oil, adding a little white wine or water for extra liquid, if needed. Set aside when done. Slice the cheese in thin slices; set aside. Prepare a pizza pan or large cookie sheet by dusting with cornmeal. Remove the dough after the punch down and roll it very thinly (no more than ¼-inch thick) over the pan. Spread with tomatoes, spices, and cheese; top with vegetables. Bake at 400°F for approximately 20 minutes, or until the bottom is a deep brown but not burned.

Prep/bake time: 1¼ hours

Quick and Easy Calzone

*Deciding what to stuff in a calzone is simply a matter of taste;
you can use almost any vegetable you like. You can also make this dish vegan
by using dairy-free egg substitute and soy cheese.*

6 SERVINGS

1	package of frozen bread/pizza dough
20	pieces sun-dried tomatoes, chopped
1	Tablespoon olive oil
1	clove garlic, crushed
1	medium onion, chopped
1	green pepper, chopped
1	cup fresh chopped broccoli
¼	cup nonfat egg substitute
½	cup light ricotta cheese
	Sprinkle of basil
¼	teaspoon salt
	Nonfat cooking spray

(continued on next page)

NUTRITIONAL ANALYSIS PER SERVING:
Serving Size: 1 slice, 2 inches thick

Calories:	240	Cholesterol:	5 mg
Protein:	11 g	Fiber:	4 g
Carbohydrate:	37 g	Sodium:	510 mg
Fat:	6 g	Calcium	91 mg
		Iron	3 mg

Diabetic Exchanges: 2 starches, 1 protein, 1 vegetable

Thaw the pizza dough by either placing it in the refrigerator overnight or leaving it at room temperature for several hours. If refrigerated, take out the dough to allow it to get to room temperature. Meanwhile, reconstitute the tomatoes in plenty of hot water and chop all of the vegetables.

In a large skillet, sauté the garlic in the oil; then add the chopped vegetables. Cook until vegetables are done (adding a little water as necessary, to prevent burning) and remove from heat.

Prepare a large cookie sheet by spraying it with cooking spray. Roll the dough in a large rectangle that is at least 9 x 13-inches. Add the egg substitute, ricotta cheese, basil and salt to the vegetable mixture. Spread the mixture on the dough from the center to the side facing you. Fold dough over to meet the side facing you, to make a 13-inch long calzone. Seal the ends well by pressing down with a wet fork.

Bake at 350°F for 25 minutes, or until the top has the color of a crust of bread and the dough is thoroughly baked.

Prep/bake time: 1¼ hours

Stuffed Baked Potatoes

This dish can be cooked in the microwave on a hot summer night.

8 STUFFED POTATO HALVES / 4 SERVINGS

1	cup chopped broccoli (fresh or frozen)
4	baking potatoes
¾	cup nonfat cottage cheese
¼	cup nonfat plain yogurt
1	Tablespoon sweet relish
2	teaspoons chives
2	teaspoons mustard
½	cup shredded lowfat Mozzarella cheese

Steam broccoli in a saucepan or steamer. Remove broccoli and microwave potatoes until fully cooked.

While potatoes are cooking, in a small bowl combine remaining ingredients, except cheese. When potatoes are done, cut lengthwise, closer to one side. Spoon out the potato pulp and add to cottage cheese mixture. Stuff the potato shells with the cottage cheese-potato pulp mixture. Microwave or bake until filling is hot. Sprinkle with cheese and cook another minute.

Prep/cook time: 20 minutes

NUTRITIONAL ANALYSIS PER SERVING:
Serving Size: 2 stuffed potato halves

Calories:	230	Cholesterol:	10 mg
Protein:	14 g	Fiber:	3 g
Carbohydrate:	39 g	Sodium:	260 mg
Fat:	3 g	Calcium	164 mg
		Iron	1 mg

Diabetic Exchanges: 2 starches, 1 protein, 1 vegetable

Potato Gnoochi

These are not at all difficult to make, but the molding of the gnoochi will take about an hour. You will need to boil all the gnoochi the same day—the dough doesn't freeze well. Be sure to accurately weigh the potatoes with a food scale.

4 SERVINGS

1	pound medium red potatoes (approximately 3)
¼	cup nonfat egg substitute
½	teaspoon salt
1	teaspoon olive oil
2	cups all-purpose flour
	Marinara Sauce (page 52)

Boil and whip the potatoes with a beater or food processor. Cool the potatoes in the refrigerator. When cooled, add the remaining ingredients; as with bread making, start with 1½ cups flour and work in remaining flour, forming a soft dough.

Separate dough into 4 quarters. With floured hands and board, roll the dough into a snake, about 1-inch in diameter. Slice the snake into 1-inch long pieces. Flour each piece, place on a fork, and roll over, leaving indentations from the fork. Curl around your thumb, leaving the piece looking like shell pasta. Place on a platter.

Drop the pieces gingerly in a large pot of boiling water. Boil only until the pieces float to the top (1½ to 2 minutes). Remove with slotted spoon.

Either serve with Marinara Sauce (page 52) or add the sauté step below.

Sauté: 1 clove minced garlic and 1 teaspoon basil in 1 Tablespoon olive oil. Stir-fry the gnoochi for 2 to 3 minutes. Serve with sauce.

Prep/cook time: 1¼ hours, not including potato baking time

NUTRITIONAL ANALYSIS PER SERVING, WITHOUT THE SAUCE:
Serving Size: 1 cup

Calories:	360	Cholesterol:	0
Protein:	11 g	Fiber:	4 g
Carbohydrate:	72 g	Sodium:	300 mg
Fat:	2 g	Calcium	24 mg
		Iron	4 mg

Diabetic Exchanges: 4 starches

Cucumber Raita

This side dish is a refreshing accompaniment to any curry or Indian meal.
Serve with pita bread.

2 CUPS / 4 SERVINGS

12 ounces (1½ cups) nonfat plain yogurt
1   cucumber, peeled and diced
2   Tablespoons chopped onion
1   tomato, chopped
2   Tablespoons sugar
½   teaspoon salt
1   teaspoon dried or 2 teaspoons fresh dill

In a small bowl, combine all ingredients. Mix well. Sprinkle with fresh dill and serve cold.

Prep time: 15 minutes

NUTRITIONAL ANALYSIS PER SERVING:
Serving Size: ½ cup

Calories:	90	Cholesterol:	0
Protein:	6 g	Fiber:	1 g
Carbohydrate:	17 g	Sodium:	340 mg
Fat:	0	Calcium	183 mg
		Iron	0

Diabetic Exchanges: 1 milk, 1 vegetable

Potato Ring with Cashews

This is a good recipe for mashed potato lovers.

1 6-CUP FLUTED TUBE PAN / 6 PORTIONS

4	large potatoes, peeled
½	teaspoon salt
1	pound of mixed vegetables, either fresh or frozen*
1	teaspoon ground ginger, preferably fresh
2	Tablespoons lemon juice
2	Tablespoons sugar
1	cup frozen corn
1	Tablespoon vegetable oil
1	teaspoon ground mustard seeds (or dry mustard)
¼	cup chopped cashew nuts
1	sweet green pepper, sliced in strips
1	sweet red pepper, sliced in strips
1	Tablespoon toasted sesame seeds
	Nonfat cooking spray

Boil, drain and mash potatoes. Add salt. Cook or steam the vegetables in a saucepan and dice any large pieces. Combine the cooked mixed vegetables with remaining ingredients (except the sliced peppers and sesame seeds) Add potatoes and mix well. Arrange pepper slices on the bottom of a 6-cup fluted tube pan that has been sprayed with cooking spray. Press the mixture into the ring. Bake for 40 minutes at 400°F. Unmold onto a serving platter and top with sesame seeds.

*You can use any combination of green beans, peas, carrots, cauliflower or zucchini.

Prep/bake time: 1½ hours

NUTRITIONAL ANALYSIS PER SERVING:			
Serving Size: 1 portion			
Calories:	270	Cholesterol:	0
Protein:	7 g	Fiber:	7 g
Carbohydrate:	47 g	Sodium:	250 mg
Fat:	6 g	Calcium	45 mg
		Iron	2 mg

Diabetic Exchanges: 2 starches, 2 vegetables, 1 fat

Potato and Green Bean Ciambotta

This Italian side dish goes well with soyburgers such as Soy-Oat Burgers on page 122 or Peanutty-Carrot Loaf on page 121.

4 1/2 CUPS / 6 SERVINGS

4	new red potatoes, unpeeled
1	Tablespoon olive oil
2	cloves garlic, crushed
½	cup white wine or vegetable broth
1	green or red pepper, cut in strips
2	cups fresh green beans, cut in half
1	Tablespoon fresh basil (or 1 teaspoon dried)
½	teaspoon salt
	Dash of pepper

Cut potatoes in quarters or small chunks and microwave for 3 to 4 minutes. Using a large skillet with a cover, sauté garlic in oil. Add potatoes and all remaining ingredients. Steam, covered, for about 15 minutes or until cooked to your preference. Add ¼ cup water if pan gets dry during steaming.

Prep/cook time: 30 minutes

NUTRITIONAL ANALYSIS PER SERVING:
Serving Size: ¾ cup

Calories:	80	Cholesterol:	0
Protein:	2 g	Fiber:	30 g
Carbohydrate:	14 g	Sodium:	180 mg
Fat:	2 g	Calcium	23 mg
		Iron	1 mg

Diabetic Exchanges: 1 starch, 1 vegetable

Kashmir Potatoes and Cauliflower

Cardamom is a hot spice which gives everyday vegetables a characteristic East Indian flavor. Add a fourth teaspoon if you prefer a less spicy dish. This is a hearty side dish, but could also serve as a main dish with soup.

8 CUPS / 8 SERVINGS

1   teaspoon oil
2   medium onions, sliced
2   garlic cloves, minced
2   pounds potatoes, peeled and chopped
      into bite-size chunks
1   quart water
1   teaspoon salt
½   teaspoon black pepper
1   pound cauliflower florets
¾   cup peas
1½   Tablespoons Curry Powder
      (page 248)

In a large saucepan, sauté onions and garlic in oil until lightly browned, adding a little water as necessary. Add potatoes and 1 quart water. Boil about 15 minutes; add remaining ingredients. Cook 15 to 20 minutes, or until sauce is thickened. You can always add a sprinkle of cornstarch to thicken faster.

Prep/cook time: 1 hour

NUTRITIONAL ANALYSIS PER SERVING:
Serving Size: 1 cup

Calories:	150	Cholesterol:	0
Protein:	5 g	Fiber:	4 g
Carbohydrate:	30 g	Sodium:	290 mg
Fat:	1 g	Calcium	29 mg
		Iron	1 mg

Diabetic Exchanges: 1 starch, 1 vegetable

Stir-Fry Sweet Potatoes

A filling and satisfying recipe,
sweet potatoes are an excellent source of beta-carotene.

3 CUPS / 4 SERVINGS

4	large fresh sweet potatoes
1	medium onion, sliced
1	sweet green pepper, sliced in strips
1	Tablespoon olive oil
1	teaspoon dried parsley
1	teaspoon dried thyme
½	teaspoon dried rosemary
½	cup white wine
¼	teaspoon salt
	Pepper to taste

Wash and scrub sweet potatoes; microwave for 3 to 4 minutes or until softened. Meanwhile, in skillet sauté onion and pepper in the oil and add herbs. Cut potatoes into bite-size cubes, add to the green pepper-onion mixture with the wine. Season with salt and pepper. Stir-fry until the potatoes are fully cooked.

Prep/cook time: 30 minutes

NUTRITIONAL ANALYSIS PER SERVING:
Serving Size: ¾ cups

Calories:	170	Cholesterol:	0
Protein:	3 g	Fiber:	4 g
Carbohydrate:	31 g	Sodium:	150 mg
Fat:	4 g	Calcium	37 mg
		Iron	1 mg

Diabetic Exchanges: 2 starches, 1 vegetable

Roasted Sweet Potatoes

This potato, when dipped in catsup, makes a good substitute for french fries.

3 CUPS / 4 SERVINGS

2 large fresh sweet potatoes, peeled and cubed
2 Tablespoons balsamic vinegar
2 Tablespoons light soy sauce
3-4 drops Louisiana hot sauce
 Nonfat cooking spray

Microwave the sweet potatoes for about 8 minutes, or until a fork pierces the potato, (but they will still be tough). Combine remaining ingredients together and brush on potatoes with a pastry brush. Spray a 7 x 11-inch baking dish with cooking spray, add potato cubes and spray them lightly with cooking spray. Roast in a 425°F oven for about 20 minutes or until they are crispy on the outside. Dip in catsup, if desired.

Prep/bake time: 35 minutes

NUTRITIONAL ANALYSIS PER SERVING:
Serving Size: ¾ cup

Calories:	80	Cholesterol:	0
Protein:	2 g	Fiber:	1 g
Carbohydrate:	18 g	Sodium:	260 mg
Fat:	0	Calcium	6 mg
		Iron	1 mg

Diabetic Exchanges: 1 starch

Grilled Vegetables with Rosemary

Grill any kind or all of the vegetables. Serve with couscous or the cold Autumn Rice Salad on page 95.

12 CUPS / 6 SERVINGS

1	zucchini or summer squash, cut into spears
1	small onion, cut in quarters
1	carrot, peeled and cut into sticks
2	small tomatoes, cut into quarters
2	portobello mushrooms, cut into chunks
1	eggplant, peeled and cut in 1-inch cubes
3	parboiled new red potatoes
2	parboiled beets, peeled and cut in chunks
1	parboiled butternut squash, peeled and cubed
2	Tablespoons olive oil
2	Tablespoons balsamic vinegar
½	teaspoon salt
	Pepper to taste
1	Tablespoon fresh rosemary, chopped

Prepare the grill. In a large bowl, place all of the vegetables you've chosen. Drizzle with olive oil, then balsamic vinegar. Mix to coat evenly. Sprinkle with salt and pepper. Then sprinkle rosemary and mix again. Place vegetables on grill; cook, while watching and turning—they will be ready at slightly different times.

Prep/grill time: 40 minutes

NUTRITIONAL ANALYSIS PER SERVING:
Serving Size: 2 cups

Calories:	130	Cholesterol:	0
Protein:	3 g	Fiber:	4 g
Carbohydrate:	21 g	Sodium:	180 mg
Fat:	4 g	Calcium	30 mg
		Iron	1 mg

Diabetic Exchanges: 1 starch, 1 vegetable, 1 fat

Vegetables Steamed in Parchment

You can use almost any favorite vegetable in this recipe; just remember to precook if necessary. Parchment paper can be found at a cooking utensil store if it is not available at your supermarket.

2 CUPS / 1 SERVING

You will need:
1   12 x 10-inch piece of tin foil
1   12 x 10-inch piece of parchment paper

1   new red baking potato, cut into ¼-inch slices
1   scallion, sliced
¼   red onion, sliced thin
1   tomato, cored, cut into wedges
4   broccoli florets
1   small zucchini, cut into spears
1   teaspoon olive oil
1   sprig fresh thyme
½   sprig fresh rosemary
¼   teaspoon salt
    Dash of pepper

Lay the foil on a flat surface; place potato slices on foil, leaving a 2-inch border all around edges. Mound the rest of the vegetables on top of the potatoes. Drizzle with the oil or brush with a pastry brush. Top with herbs and spices.

Place parchment over the vegetables. Carefully crimp the foil over the paper. Seal tightly, so no steam escapes.

Bake at 400°F about 20 minutes or until paper turns golden brown.

Prep/bake time: 40 minutes

NUTRITIONAL ANALYSIS PER SERVING:
Serving Size: 2 cups

Calories:	240	Cholesterol:	0
Protein:	6 g	Fiber:	6 g
Carbohydrate:	46 g	Sodium:	290 mg
Fat:	4 g	Calcium	42 mg
		Iron	2 mg

Diabetic Exchanges: 1 starch, 4 vegetables, 1 fat

String Beans with Sesame Dressing

Fresh beans add a crispier texture, but frozen will work as well.
Use either spicy or plain mustard.

9 CUPS / 12 SERVINGS

3	pounds fresh string beans
2	Tablespoons sesame seeds
½	cup chopped red bell pepper
½	cup chopped yellow bell pepper
⅓	cup red wine vinegar
¼	cup soy sauce
1	Tablespoon hot or Dijon mustard
1	Tablespoon sugar
⅓	cup sesame oil
3-4	cloves garlic*
¼	cup chopped scallions

Wash and trim ends of beans; cut in half. In large saucepan, steam the beans until crisp-tender. Place beans in ice water, then drain and place in a large bowl. Combine dressing ingredients while the beans are cooking; toss dressing with the cooled beans. Serve cold.

*Precook the garlic as follows: Wrap in foil and bake for 15 minutes at 350°F; then mash into the oil. If you prefer the sharper fresh flavor, simply mince garlic into the oil.

Prep/cook time: 40 minutes

NUTRITIONAL ANALYSIS PER SERVING:
Serving Size: ¾ cup

Calories:	120	Cholesterol:	0
Protein:	5 g	Fiber:	5 g
Carbohydrate:	13 g	Sodium:	280 mg
Fat:	5 g	Calcium	62 mg
		Iron	2 mg

Diabetic Exchanges: 2 vegetables, 1 fat

Caponata

Use as a side dish, main dish, or appetizer.
Cocoa powder adds a special flavor to the eggplant.

3 CUPS / 4 SERVINGS

1   large eggplant, peeled
2   hard boiled egg whites
1   medium onion, chopped
1   Tablespoon olive oil
½   cup white wine
2   Tablespoons tomato paste
1   Tablespoon sugar
¼   teaspoon unsweetened cocoa powder
1   Tablespoon fresh basil
     (or ½ Tablespoon dried)
2   Tablespoons pine nuts (optional)
1   fresh tomato, chopped

Slice the eggplant in 1-inch thick slices. Salt the slices and place in a colander for about 30 minutes to let the juices drain. (It helps to put a weight of some kind on the eggplant.)

Meanwhile, boil the eggs and chop the onion. When the eggplant has drained, rinse and chop into small bite-size pieces.

In a large skillet, sauté the onion in oil. Add wine and tomato paste. Combine sugar with the cocoa powder; add basil. Add this mixture to onion. Add pine nuts, if desired. Simmer 20 minutes, or until eggplant is fully cooked. Remove from heat, add tomato, and serve hot or cold with fresh bread.

Prep/cook time: 1 hour

NUTRITIONAL ANALYSIS PER SERVING:
Serving Size: ¾ cup

Calories:	110	Cholesterol:	0
Protein:	3 g	Fiber:	1 g
Carbohydrate:	13 g	Sodium:	270 mg
Fat:	5 g	Calcium	15 mg
		Iron	1 mg

Diabetic Exchanges: 2 vegetables, 1 fat

Chapter 10

Breads

Breads

Oatmeal Bread

This high protein bread is great for sandwiches or toast.

2 8 X 4-INCH LOAVES / 32 SLICES

1½ cups dry rolled oats
3   cups hot water
2   Tablespoons molasses
1   teaspoon salt
½   cup nonfat dry milk powder
2   Tablespoons oil
2   packages yeast (rapid rise)
¾   cup warm water
6½ to 7½ cups enriched white flour
      Nonfat cooking spray
Glaze:
1   egg white
1   Tablespoon water

Preheat oven to 350°F.

In a large mixing bowl, add rolled oats to the 3 cups hot water. Add molasses, salt, dry milk powder and oil. Mix and let stand until luke warm. In a small bowl, add yeast to the ¾ cup of warm water, stirring together.

Add yeast to the cooled oatmeal mixture. Add flour, one cup at a time, until the dough can be handled.

By hand, knead in the remaining flour until the dough is smooth and elastic, adding a little more flour if the dough is sticky.

Place dough in bowl sprayed with nonfat cooking spray. Spray the top lightly with cooking spray. Cover; let rise in warm place until light and doubled, about 30 minutes. *(continued on next page)*

NUTRITIONAL ANALYSIS PER SERVING:
Serving Size: 1 slice

Calories:	72	Cholesterol:	0
Protein:	2 g	Fiber:	1 g
Carbohydrate:	14 g	Sodium:	64 mg
Fat:	1 g	Calcium	15 mg
		Iron	1 mg

Diabetic Exchanges: 1 starch

Generously spray two 8 x 4-inch loaf pans with cooking spray. Punch down dough; divide into 2 loaf pans. Brush with egg white and water glaze. Cover; let rise until doubled in size, about 30 minutes. Bake at 350°F for 50 to 55 minutes, or until crust is brown.

Prep/bake time: 2 hours

Anadama Bread

This is a sweet bread recipe appropriate for bread machines and makes terrific toast! If you don't have a bread machine, combine yeast with the water and molasses in a small bowl, then continue as you would to make any homemade bread.

ONE 8 X 4-INCH LOAF / 16 SLICES

Add to the bread machine in the following order:

1   **cup warm water**
¼   **cup molasses**
2   **teaspoons canola or safflower oil**
¼   **cup nonfat egg substitute**
½   **cup cornmeal**
2   **Tablespoons sugar**
½   **teaspoon salt**
3   **cups all-purpose or bread flour**
1½   **teaspoons (1 package) yeast**
      Nonfat cooking spray

Start the machine and run through the cycle. If you prefer, you can take the bread out after the punch-down time (about 45 minutes) and place in an 8 x 4-inch loaf pan sprayed with nonfat cooking spray. Let rise until double. Bake at 350°F for about 50 minutes, or until bread sounds hollow when you tap it. **Prep/bake time: 2½ hours**

NUTRITIONAL ANALYSIS PER SERVING:
Serving Size: 1 slice

Calories:	110	Cholesterol:	0
Protein:	3 g	Fiber:	0
Carbohydrate:	22 g	Sodium:	65 mg
Fat:	1 g	Calcium:	18 mg
		Iron	1 mg

Diabetic Exchanges: 1 starch

Rye Bread

Homemade bread takes time, but is so worth it!

TWO 8 X 4-INCH LOAVES / 32 SLICES

2   packages dry yeast (preferably rapid rise)
½   cup warm water
3   cups rye flour
½   cup molasses
3   Tablespoons plus 1 teaspoon canola oil
1   teaspoon salt
1½   cups hot water
3 to 3½ cups enriched white flour

Glaze:
1   egg white
1   Tablespoon water

Soften yeast in warm water; set aside. In a large mixing bowl, combine rye flour, molasses, 3 tablespoons oil and salt. Add hot water and stir. Cool to lukewarm and add yeast mixture. Stir in two cups of white flour and mix. Add remaining flour, by hand, and knead ten minutes. Continue to add pinches of flour until dough is smooth and elastic. Smooth a teaspoon of oil over the top of the dough and flip the dough over in the bowl. Cover with warm, wet cloth and let rise in a warm place until light and doubled in size. Lightly oil two 8 x 4-inch loaf pans. Punch dough down and separate into two loaves. Let rise until doubled in size. Prepare glaze by mixing egg white with water. Brush loaves with egg white glaze and bake at 350°F for 30 to 45 minutes or until the loaf sounds hollow when you tap it.
For bread machines: Cut all ingredients in half; adding water first and yeast last. Remove after punch down time (45 minutes) and place in one oiled loaf pan. Continue directions accordingly. **Prep/cook time: 1½ hours**

NUTRITIONAL ANALYSIS PER SERVING:
Serving Size: 1 slice

Calories:	75	Cholesterol:	0
Protein:	2 g	Fiber:	1 g
Carbohydrate:	14 g	Sodium:	70 mg
Fat:	1 g	Calcium	13 mg
		Iron	1 mg

Diabetic Exchanges: 1 starch

Cinnamon Raisin Bagels

Homemade bagels go stale quickly, freeze remaining bagels when they cool.

10 BAGELS

1	package active dry yeast (rapid rise)
1	cup warm water
1	Tablespoon molasses
2	Tablespoons sugar
3	cups all-purpose flour
½	teaspoon cinnamon
1	teaspoon salt
¼	cup raisins
	Nonfat cooking spray
1	gallon water
1	teaspoon vegetable oil

Preheat oven to 350°F. In a large mixing bowl, combine yeast, warm water, and molasses; allow this to set for 5 minutes.

In a separate bowl, combine sugar, flour, cinnamon, salt, and raisins. Add this mixture to the yeast-molasses mixture. Blend well.

By hand, knead dough until smooth and elastic, about 10 minutes. Add more flour if dough is sticky. Cover; let rest 10 minutes. Cut into 10 portions; shape each into a smooth ball. Punch a hole into the center of each with your finger. Pull gently to make a 1½ -inch hole.

Place on a lightly sprayed cookie sheet. Cover; let rise in a warm place until doubled, about 20 minutes.

Heat 1 gallon water with a teaspoon of oil to boiling. Drop bagels, one at a time into the water and cook 5 bagels at a time for 3 to 4 minutes, turning once. Drain on paper towels. *(continued on next page)*

NUTRITIONAL ANALYSIS PER SERVING:
Serving Size: 1 bagel

Calories:	180	Cholesterol:	0
Protein:	4 g	Fiber:	2 g
Carbohydrate:	40 g	Sodium:	230 mg
Fat:	0	Calcium	17 mg
		Iron	2 mg

Diabetic Exchanges: 2 starches

Place on sprayed cookie sheet. Bake at 350°F (center of oven) for 10 minutes; increase heat to 400°F and bake for an additional 10 minutes.

Directions for bread machines: If you wish to start the dough in a bread machine, add the ingredients in the order given, except add the yeast last. Start the machine and run for about 30 minutes. After the dough is mixed and is warm, remove dough from the machine and follow directions accordingly, adding a little more flour if sticky.

Prep/cook time: 1¾ hours

Corn Bread

Corn bread complements chili, baked beans, or almost any Mexican dish.

9-INCH SQUARE BAKING DISH / 12 PORTIONS

1½ cups all-purpose flour
¾   cup cornmeal
2   teaspoons baking powder
⅓   cup sugar
1   teaspoon salt
2   egg whites, slightly beaten
3   Tablespoons vegetable oil
1½ cups skim milk
    Nonfat cooking spray

Preheat oven to 400°F. Spray 9-inch square baking dish with nonfat cooking spray. In a mixing bowl, combine flour, cornmeal, baking powder, sugar and salt. Add remaining ingredients and stir only until blended. Pour into prepared 9-inch square baking dish. Bake at 400°F for 20 to 25 minutes or until toothpick comes out clean.

Prep/bake time: 40 minutes

NUTRITIONAL ANALYSIS PER SERVING:
Serving Size: 1 portion

Calories:	150	Cholesterol:	0
Protein:	4 g	Fiber:	1 g
Carbohydrate:	26 g	Sodium:	200 mg
Fat:	3 g	Calcium	41 mg
		Iron	1 mg

Diabetic Exchanges: 2 starches

Pineapple Cornbread

This variation works well as a breakfast bread and stays moist for days.

9-INCH SQUARE BAKING DISH / 12 PORTIONS

1¼   cups all-purpose flour
¾   cup cornmeal
¼   cup sugar
2   teaspoons baking powder
½   teaspoon salt

¾   cup skim milk
3   Tablespoons vegetable oil
1   8-ounce can crushed pineapple, with juice
2   egg whites (or ¼ cup nonfat egg substitute)
    Nonfat cooking spray

Heat oven to 400°F. Lightly spray 9-inch square baking dish with cooking spray. In a medium bowl, combine first 5 dry ingredients. Stir in remaining ingredients and mix until moistened (do not over-mix). Pour batter into prepared baking dish.

Bake at 400°F for 25 to 30 minutes or until golden brown. Cool on a wire rack.

Prep/bake time: 45 minutes

NUTRITIONAL ANALYSIS PER SERVING:
Serving Size: 1 portion

Calories:	146	Cholesterol:	0
Protein:	3 g	Fiber:	1 g
Carbohydrate:	24 g	Sodium:	106 mg
Fat:	4 g	Calcium	24 mg
		Iron	1 mg

Diabetic Exchanges: 1 starch, 1 fat

Fat Free One-Rise Cinnamon Bread

This bread is wonderful toasted and served with apple jelly.

TWO 8 X 4-INCH LOAVES / 32 SLICES

2½ cups warm water
2 packages yeast (preferably fast-rising)
½ cup instant nonfat dry milk
2 Tablespoons sugar
2 teaspoons salt
7 to 7½ cups enriched white flour

2 Tablespoons brown sugar
2 teaspoons cinnamon
Nonfat cooking spray

In a small bowl, mix brown sugar and cinnamon together; set aside. Spray two 8 x 4-inch loaf pans with nonfat cooking spray. Measure water into a large mixing bowl and sprinkle yeast over water. Add dry milk, sugar, and salt. Add half of the flour and mix. By hand, gradually stir in the remaining flour to form a stiff dough. Knead dough on a floured surface until smooth and elastic, about 7 to 8 minutes.

Split dough in half. Roll each into an 8 x 6-inch rectangle. Sprinkle both rectangles with the cinnamon-sugar mixture. Roll tightly (as in a jelly roll fashion) and pinch edges to seal. Place each roll into a prepared loaf pan, seam side down.

Cover and let rise in warm place till doubled in size, 30 to 60 minutes. Bake for 35 to 40 minutes at 375°F. Immediately remove from pan. Serve warm.

Prep/bake time: 2 hours

NUTRITIONAL ANALYSIS PER SERVING:
Serving Size: 1 slice

Calories:	74	Cholesterol:	0
Protein:	2 g	Fiber:	0
Carbohydrate:	18 g	Sodium:	72 mg
Fat:	0	Calcium	9 mg
		Iron	1 mg

Diabetic Exchanges: 1 starch

Cranberry Tea Braid

Make rolls from the dough with a cookie cutter and place the cranberry filling on top as an option to the braid. Cranberry, blueberry or raspberry preserves can be substituted for the filling.

1 BRAID / 12 SLICES

Dough:

¼   cup warm water
1   package dry yeast (1½ teaspoons)
¾   cup warm skim milk
¼   cup sugar
1   teaspoon salt
¼   cup nonfat egg substitute
1   Tablespoon margarine
3½ cups bread or all-purpose flour
    Nonfat cooking spray

Filling:

½   cup fresh cranberries
¼   cup sugar
¼   cup water
1   teaspoon cornstarch

Dough: Dissolve yeast in the warm water. The water should be lukewarm, not hot. Add milk, sugar, salt, egg substitute, and margarine; stir until blended. Add 3 cups of the flour and knead in, by hand, the last ½ cup or just add enough to make a smooth and elastic dough. You may need to add a little more flour if the dough is sticky. Knead 5 to 8 minutes. Place in a lightly oiled bowl, cover with plastic wrap or towel. Let rise on a preheated stove until doubled in size. *(continued on next page)*

NUTRITIONAL ANALYSIS PER SERVING:
Serving Size: 1 slice or roll

Calories:	190	Cholesterol:	0
Protein:	5 g	Fiber:	2 g
Carbohydrate:	38 g	Sodium:	200 mg
Fat:	2 g	Calcium	28 mg
		Iron	2 mg

Diabetic Exchanges: 2 starches, 1 fruit

Filling: Prepare filling by placing all ingredients into a saucepan and heating until it has the consistency of a jam. Remove from heat and set aside.

Braid: Punch dough down; roll dough into a 12 x 9-inch rectangle. Spread a thin layer of the filling down the center. You only need a small amount of the filling; save the rest to use as jam.

Cut 12 (1-inch) strips on either side of the jam. Fold both outer strips into the center at a slight angle. Slide the braid onto an sprayed cookie sheet and let rise until doubled in size.

Brush braid with additional egg substitute. Bake at 375°F for 20 minutes or until golden brown on top.

Prep/bake time: 2 to 2½ hours

Banana Bread

This makes a nice gift bread to take along when visiting friends or relatives.

ONE 8 X 4-INCH LOAF / 16 SLICES

1½   cups sifted all-purpose flour
1   teaspoon baking soda
½   teaspoon salt
1   cup sugar
2   teaspoons margarine
¼   cup nonfat egg substitute
3   ripe bananas, mashed
      Nonfat cooking spray

Preheat oven to 350°F. Spray and flour bottom of 8 x 4-inch loaf pan. In a large bowl, mix flour, baking soda and salt. In a small bowl, blend sugar, margarine, egg substitute, and mashed bananas until creamy. Add the banana mixture to the flour mixture and stir just until well blended.

Pour batter into prepared loaf pan. Bake in a preheated 350°F oven for 1 hour or until top springs back when touched. Let cool before slicing.

Prep/bake time: 1½ hours

NUTRITIONAL ANALYSIS PER SERVING:
Serving Size: 1 slice

Calories:	112	Cholesterol:	0
Protein:	2 g	Fiber:	1 g
Carbohydrate:	26 g	Sodium:	80 mg
Fat:	0	Calcium	5 mg
		Iron	1 mg

Diabetic Exchanges: 2 starches

Italian Tea Biscuits

These biscuits make great afternoon snacks as well as delightful breakfast treats.

12 BISCUITS

Dough:
1¾ cups all-purpose flour, divided
1   Tablespoon baking powder
½   teaspoon salt
1   Tablespoon sugar
1   Tablespoon safflower or canola oil
½   cup skim milk

Filling:
¼   cup part-skim ricotta cheese
2   Tablespoons sugar
1   teaspoon fresh chives
     Nonfat cooking spray

Preheat oven to 400°F. Spray 9 x 13-inch baking dish with nonfat cooking spray. In a large bowl, combine 1½ cups flour, baking powder, salt and sugar. Using fork or pastry blender, cut in oil until consistency of coarse-meal. Add milk; stir with fork until a soft dough forms. Sprinkle in a little more flour, until you get a biscuit dough consistency. Turn dough onto a floured surface; sprinkle lightly with flour. Knead gently until no longer sticky. Roll into a 12 x 18-inch rectangle.

Combine filling ingredients together and spread over dough. Start rolling dough lengthwise (in jelly roll style) to make a long roll, sprinkling flour as necessary. Pinch edges to seal. Cut roll into 12 portions as follows: cut the roll in half; then cut each half in half again. Cut each quarter into thirds, making 12 rolls. *(continued on next page)*

NUTRITIONAL ANALYSIS PER SERVING:
Serving Size: 1 biscuit

Calories:	100	Cholesterol:	0
Protein:	3 g	Fiber:	1 g
Carbohydrate:	18 g	Sodium:	100 mg
Fat:	2 g	Calcium	29 mg
		Iron	1 mg

Diabetic Exchanges: 1 starch

Place rolls cut-side down in a 9 x 13-inch baking dish. Round off tops with a knife or spatula. Bake for approximately 20 minutes at 400°F in center of oven. Watch after 15 minutes to avoid burning the bottoms.

Prep/bake time: 1 hour

Corn-Blue Muffins

Large or medium-sized frozen unsweetened blueberries work well in this recipe. This makes 10 muffins; so you may want to fill the two empty cups with water.

10 MUFFINS

1½ cups all-purpose flour
½ cup sugar
¼ cup cornmeal
1 Tablespoon baking powder
½ teaspoon salt

¼ cup nonfat egg substitute
2 Tablespoons canola or safflower oil
2 Tablespoons light corn syrup
¾ cup skim milk
½ teaspoon vanilla extract
1 cup frozen unsweetened blueberries
Nonfat cooking spray

Preheat oven to 400°F. Spray bottoms of muffin cups with cooking spray or line with paper baking cups. In a large bowl, mix together first 5 ingredients. Stir in remaining ingredients just until dry ingredients are moistened. Spoon batter into prepared muffin cups, filling ⅔ full. Bake for approximately 20 minutes at 400°F in center of oven. Cool on a wire rack.

Prep/bake time: 45 minutes

NUTRITIONAL ANALYSIS PER SERVING:
Serving Size: 1 muffin

Calories:	170	Cholesterol:	0
Protein:	3 g	Fiber:	1 g
Carbohydrate:	33 g	Sodium:	130 mg
Fat:	3 g	Calcium	30 mg
		Iron	1 mg

Diabetic Exchanges: 2 starches

Bran Muffins with Applesauce

These muffins are high in fiber and contain one-fourth the fat found in bakery bran muffins.

12 MUFFINS

1   cup 100% bran cereal
⅔   cup skim milk

1   cup all-purpose flour
1   Tablespoon baking powder
½   teaspoon salt
¼   cup brown sugar
1   teaspoon cinnamon

¼   cup nonfat egg substitute
2   Tablespoons oil
¾   cup applesauce
    Nonfat cooking spray

Preheat oven to 400°F. Spray bottoms of muffin cups with cooking spray or line with paper baking cups. In a small mixing bowl, combine the bran cereal with the milk. In a large mixing bowl, mix the next 5 dry ingredients. Add the egg substitute, oil, and applesauce to the cereal. Add the cereal-applesauce mixture to the flour mixture. Stir until dry ingredients are moistened. Spoon batter into prepared cups, filling ⅔ full.

Bake for approximately 20 minutes at 400°F in center of oven or until lightly browned.

Prep/bake time: 45 minutes

NUTRITIONAL ANALYSIS PER SERVING:
Serving Size: 1 muffin

Calories:	100	Cholesterol:	0
Protein:	3 g	Fiber:	3 g
Carbohydrate:	18 g	Sodium:	270 mg
Fat:	2 g	Calcium	96 mg
		Iron	1 mg

Diabetic Exchanges: 1 starch

Multi-Grain Pumpkin Muffins

The mashed pumpkin in these muffins add fat-free moisture and sweetness; and, like other orange-colored vegetables, it's rich in protective anti-oxidants.

12 MUFFINS

1	cup whole-wheat flour
1	cup white flour
⅔	cup brown sugar
1	Tablespoon baking powder
2	teaspoons cinnamon
½	teaspoon salt
½	cup rolled oats
1½	cups skim milk
1	cup canned pumpkin
1	Tablespoon vegetable oil
2	egg whites (or ¼ cup nonfat egg substitute)
	Cooking Spray

Preheat oven to 400°F. Spray bottoms of muffin cups with cooking spray or line with paper baking cups. In a large mixing bowl, mix first 6 dry ingredients. In another bowl, combine the oats, milk, pumpkin, oil, and egg whites. Add the milk-pumpkin mixture to the dry ingredients and stir just until dry ingredients are moistened.

Spoon batter into prepared muffin cups, filling ⅔ full. Bake muffins at 400°F for 25 minutes or until a toothpick comes out clean.

Prep/cook time: 45 minutes

NUTRITIONAL ANALYSIS PER SERVING:
Serving Size: 1 muffin

Calories:	150	Cholesterol:	0
Protein:	5 g	Fiber:	2 g
Carbohydrate:	28 g	Sodium:	110 mg
Fat:	2 g	Calcium	57 mg
		Iron	1 mg

Diabetic Exchanges: 2 starches

Strawberry Muffins

*Fresh strawberries are recommended for these muffins, but you can use frozen
if you drain the juice from the thawed berries first.*

12 MUFFINS

2   cups all-purpose flour
½   cup sugar
1   Tablespoon baking powder
½   teaspoon salt

2   egg whites (or ¼ cup nonfat egg substitute)
½   cup nonfat plain yogurt (or skim milk)
2   Tablespoons safflower or canola oil
⅔   cup (about 8 or 9) mashed strawberries
    Nonfat cooking spray
1   Tablespoon sugar for topping

Preheat oven to 400°F. Spray bottoms of muffin cups with cooking spray or
line with paper baking cups. In a mixing bowl, blend together first 4 dry
ingredients. In a small bowl, mix together egg whites, yogurt, oil, and
strawberries. Add yogurt mixture to dry ingredients, stirring just until dry
ingredients are moistened. Spoon batter into prepared muffin cups, filling
⅔ full. Sprinkle with sugar. Bake at 400°F for 25 minutes or until a toothpick comes out clean.

Prep/bake time: 45 minutes

NUTRITIONAL ANALYSIS PER SERVING: *Serving Size: 1 muffin*			
Calories:	140	Cholesterol:	0
Protein:	3 g	Fiber:	3 g
Carbohydrate:	26 g	Sodium:	110 mg
Fat:	3 g	Calcium	25
		Iron	1 mg

Diabetic Exchanges: 1 starch, 1 fruit

Oatmeal Banana Muffins

These muffins are great for breakfast, yet sweet enough to serve as a dessert.

12 MUFFINS

1   cup skim milk
1   cup rolled oats
3   Tablespoons vegetable oil
2   egg whites
1   large or 2 small bananas

½   cup brown sugar
1   Tablespoon baking powder
1   teaspoon cinnamon
½   teaspoon salt
1   cup all-purpose flour
     Nonfat cooking spray

Preheat oven to 400°F. Spray bottoms of muffin cups with cooking spray or line with paper baking cups. In a large bowl, combine first 5 ingredients. Add brown sugar, baking powder, cinnamon, and salt. Blend well. Add flour, stirring just until flour is moistened. Spoon batter into prepared muffin cups, filling ⅔ full. Bake at 400°F for 25 minutes or until a toothpick comes out clean.

Prep/bake time: 45 minutes

NUTRITIONAL ANALYSIS PER SERVING:
Serving Size: 1 muffin

Calories:	130	Cholesterol:	0
Protein:	4 g	Fiber:	1 g
Carbohydrate:	22 g	Sodium:	110 mg
Fat:	3 g	Calcium	36 mg
		Iron	1 mg

Diabetic Exchanges: 1 starch, 1 fruit

Whole-Grain Strawberry Pancakes

These tasty lowfat pancakes contain one-fourth the fat of traditional pancakes made with oil.

8 PANCAKES

½ cup skim milk
½ cup 1% cottage cheese
½ cup nonfat egg substitute
1 Tablespoon sugar
4 strawberries, chopped small
(or ¼ cup raspberries)

¾ cup whole-wheat flour
Nonfat cooking spray

Heat griddle or nonstick skillet to medium-high heat (375°F). In a large mixing bowl, combine first 5 ingredients. Stir well. Stir in flour just until large lumps disappear.

Spray skillet with nonfat cooking spray. A few drops of water sprinkled on the skillet will sizzle and bead when heat is just right. Pour the batter about ¼ cup at a time onto the skillet. Bake until bubbles form and edges start to dry; turn and bake other side.

Top with light maple syrup or strawberry jam.

Prep/cook time: 30 minutes

NUTRITIONAL ANALYSIS PER SERVING:
Serving Size: 2 pancakes

Calories:	153	Cholesterol:	0
Protein:	12 g	Fiber:	3 g
Carbohydrate:	22 g	Sodium:	190 mg
Fat:	2 g	Calcium	81 mg
		Iron	2 mg

Diabetic Exchanges: 1 starch, 1 protein, 1 fruit

Chapter 11

Desserts

Desserts

Mocha Cookies

These cookies satisfy anyone's desire for a tasty chocolate cookie.

18 COOKIES

1½ cups all-purpose flour
½ teaspoon baking soda (mix into flour)
⅔ cup sugar
3 Tablespoons unsweetened cocoa powder
1 teaspoon vanilla extract
¼ cup nonfat egg substitute
¼ cup kahlua or black coffee
2 Tablespoons vegetable oil
2 Tablespoons light corn syrup
Nonfat cooking spray

Preheat oven to 350°F. In a large bowl, combine flour, baking soda, sugar, and cocoa. Add remaining ingredients; blend until smooth.

Spray cookie sheet with cooking spray. Drop by rounded teaspoonfuls onto cookie sheet, 1-inch apart, making 18 cookies. Bake at 350°F for 10 to 12 minutes, or until slightly browned on the bottom. Remove from cookie sheet and place on wire rack.

Prep/bake time: 45 minutes

NUTRITIONAL ANALYSIS PER SERVING:
Serving Size: 1 cookie

Calories:	50	Cholesterol:	0
Protein:	0	Fiber:	0
Carbohydrate:	10 g	Sodium:	60 mg
Fat:	1 g	Calcium	4 mg
		Iron	1 mg

Diabetic Exchanges: 1 starch

Meringues

This heavenly cookie has been a fat-free favorite for decades.

18 COOKIES

6	egg whites
¼	teaspoon salt
¼	teaspoon cream of tartar
1	cup sugar
1	teaspoon vanilla extract
	Colored sprinkles (optional)

Preheat oven to 250°F. Line cookie sheet with tin foil. In a medium bowl, beat egg whites for a few minutes until frothy (make sure there is no egg yolk mixed in). Add salt and cream of tartar; continue beating until peaks form. Gradually beat in sugar and vanilla.

Drop by teaspoonfuls, 2 inches apart, onto prepared cookie sheet. Cookies will be about 2 inches in diameter. Add colored sprinkles, if desired.

Bake at 250°F for 45 minutes or until cookies are light golden brown on top. Turn off oven, but leave cookies inside for another 30 minutes.

Prep/cook time: 1¾ hours

NUTRITIONAL ANALYSIS PER SERVING:
Serving Size: 1 cookie

Calories:	40	Cholesterol:	0
Protein:	1 g	Fiber:	0
Carbohydrate:	8 g	Sodium:	65 mg
Fat:	0	Calcium	1 mg
		Iron	0

Diabetic Exchanges: 1 starch

Branapple Cookies

These cookies are kept soft and moist by the applesauce.

32 COOKIES

1	cup 40% bran flakes
1	cup applesauce
¼	cup light margarine
2	egg whites (or ¼ cup nonfat egg substitute)
2	cups all-purpose flour
1	teaspoon baking powder
1	cup sugar
1	teaspoon cinnamon
¼	teaspoon salt
	Nonfat cooking spray

Preheat oven to 350°F. In a mixing bowl, combine bran flakes with applesauce. Add margarine and egg whites; mix well.

In a separate bowl, combine remaining ingredients. Add the cereal mixture to the flour mixture and blend together. Drop by teaspoonfuls onto a cookie sheet sprayed with cooking spray. Bake at 350°F for approximately 15 minutes or until lightly browned.

Prep/bake time: 45 minutes

NUTRITIONAL ANALYSIS PER SERVING:
Serving Size: 1 cookie

Calories:	70	Cholesterol:	0
Protein:	1 g	Fiber:	1 g
Carbohydrate:	15 g	Sodium:	50 mg
Fat:	1 g	Calcium	4 mg
		Iron	1 mg

Diabetic Exchanges: 1 starch

Oatmeal Cookies

Less oil makes these cookies a healthy option; the dates keep them moist.

32 COOKIES

1   cup all-purpose flour
2   cups rolled oats
2   teaspoon baking powder
½   teaspoon salt
½   cup sugar

¾   cup chopped pitted dates
¾   cup water, divided
½   cup nonfat egg substitute
¼   cup safflower or canola oil
     Nonfat cooking spray

Preheat oven to 325°F. In a large mixing bowl, mix first 5 dry ingredients; set aside. In a small saucepan, combine dates with ½ cup of the water. Heat, stirring constantly, for about 4 to 5 minutes until dates soften and start to form a purée. Remove from heat, add remaining water to cool the mixture.

Add date mixture, egg substitute, and oil to the flour-rolled oats mixture. Mix well and drop by rounded teaspoonfuls onto a cookie sheet sprayed with cooking spray. Bake at 325°F approximately 12 minutes or until lightly browned on top.

Prep/bake time: 1 hour

NUTRITIONAL ANALYSIS PER SERVING:
Serving Size: 1 cookie

Calories:	70	Cholesterol:	0
Protein:	2 g	Fiber:	1 g
Carbohydrate:	12 g	Sodium:	40 mg
Fat:	2 g	Calcium	6 mg
		Iron	1 mg

Diabetic Exchanges: 1 starch

Raspberry Almond Cookies

I use almond-flavored liqueur to add moistness and impart a subtle almond flavor. The jam I use is an "all fruit" type, but I'm sure any kind will work.

24 COOKIES

1¾ cups all-purpose flour
1   teaspoon baking powder
½   teaspoon baking soda
½   cup sugar
¼   teaspoon salt

¼   cup nonfat egg substitute
¼   cup light corn syrup
3   Tablespoons light margarine
2   Tablespoons amaretto
1   teaspoon vanilla extract
     Nonfat cooking spray
¼   cup raspberry jam

In a deep bowl, combine the first 5 ingredients. Add the remaining ingredients, except the cooking spray and jam, and mix vigorously until well blended. Place the dough in the freezer or refrigerator for about 10 minutes to cool. Meanwhile, take out the jam and preheat oven to 375°F. Remove the dough from the refrigerator when cold.

Roll dough into 24 walnut-size balls and place onto a cookie sheet sprayed with cooking spray. Using a clean ½ teaspoon measuring spoon, make a "thumbprint" indentation in each cookie with the spoon and place about ¼ teaspoon jam in the center.

Bake for 10 minutes at 375°F; be sure to check the bottoms to prevent burning. **Prep/bake time: 45 minutes**

NUTRITIONAL ANALYSIS PER SERVING:
Serving Size: 1 cookie

Calories:	60	Cholesterol:	0
Protein:	1 g	Fiber:	0
Carbohydrate:	13 g	Sodium:	35 mg
Fat:	1 g	Calcium	3 mg
		Iron	1 mg

Diabetic Exchanges: 1 starch

Almond Biscotti

This is a lowfat version of the Italian cookie that can contain as much as 10 grams of fat in the commercial varieties.

18 COOKIES

2½ cups all-purpose flour
⅔ cup sugar
½ teaspoon baking soda
1 teaspoon baking powder

¼ cup skim milk
¼ cup amaretto liqueur
½ cup nonfat egg substitute
2 Tablespoons vegetable oil
½ teaspoon almond extract (or vanilla extract)
Nonfat cooking spray

Preheat oven to 350°F. In a large bowl, mix first 4 ingredients. In a small bowl, combine remaining ingredients. Add liquid ingredient mixture to dry ingredients. Mix together to make a stiff cookie dough, using your hands to mix and knead a little at the end.

Spray a cookie sheet with cooking spray. Spread the dough out in a long roll (about 18 inches) on the cookie sheet. Flatten the dough a little on top.

Bake for 20 minutes at 350°F; checking after 15 minutes to make sure the bottom doesn't get too browned. Remove and allow to cool for 1 hour. Slice 1-inch thick slices and turn on their side on the cookie sheet. Bake for 8 minutes on each side at 325°F. Cool and serve.

Prep/bake time: 1 hour, not including cooling time.

NUTRITIONAL ANALYSIS PER SERVING:
Serving Size: 1 cookie

Calories:	101	Cholesterol:	0
Protein:	3 g	Fiber:	1 g
Carbohydrate:	21 g	Sodium:	20 mg
Fat:	1 g	Calcium	11 mg
		Iron	1 mg

Diabetic Exchanges: 1 starch

Grapenut® Cookies

I recommend freezing these cookies when they cool to keep them fresh. However, if they start to get stale, you can combine 2 or 3 cookies with skim milk in a cereal bowl for a delicious late night snack.

3 6   C O O K I E S

½ cup Grapenuts® cereal
¾ cup apple juice
3 egg whites
¼ cup light corn syrup
1 cup all-purpose flour
1 cup rolled oats
1 teaspoon baking powder
¼ cup sugar
½ teaspoon cinnamon
½ cup raisins (optional)
Nonfat cooking spray

Preheat oven to 375°F. In a small bowl, soak the Grapenuts® in the apple juice. Add egg whites and corn syrup.

In a larger bowl, combine the remaining ingredients and add the Grapenuts® mixture. Stir only until well blended. Drop by rounded teaspoonfuls onto a cookie sheet sprayed with cooking spray.

Bake at 375°F for about 10 minutes until lightly browned.

Prep/bake time: 40 minutes

NUTRITIONAL ANALYSIS PER SERVING:
Serving Size: 1 cookie

Calories:	50	Cholesterol:	0
Protein:	1 g	Fiber:	1 g
Carbohydrate:	11 g	Sodium:	10 mg
Fat:	0	Calcium	5 mg
		Iron	0

Diabetic Exchanges: 1 starch

Mocha Brownies

These are delicious enough to serve to company and very low in fat.

8-INCH SQUARE BAKING DISH / 16 BROWNIES

¼ cup light margarine
1 cup sugar
½ cup nonfat egg substitute
¼ cup brewed black coffee
⅔ cup nonfat sour cream
1 teaspoon real vanilla extract
1 teaspoon baking powder
½ cup unsweetened cocoa powder
1 cup all-purpose flour
Powdered sugar for top, if desired
Nonfat cooking spray

Heat oven to 350°F. Spray 8-inch square baking dish with cooking spray. In a mixing bowl, combine margarine and sugar together. Add egg substitute and beat well. Add remaining ingredients, except powdered sugar. Blend well but do not over-mix. Spread in prepared baking dish. Bake at 350°F for 25 to 30 minutes or until a toothpick comes out clean. If desired, sprinkle with powdered sugar. Cool on wire rack; cut into bars.

Prep/bake time: 1 hour

NUTRITIONAL ANALYSIS PER SERVING:
Serving Size: 1 brownie

Calories:	110	Cholesterol:	0
Protein:	3 g	Fiber:	0
Carbohydrate:	23 g	Sodium:	60 mg
Fat:	1 g	Calcium	22 mg
		Iron	1 mg

Diabetic Exchanges: 1 starch

Shelley's Apple Squares

These wholesome nutritious ingredients combine to make a sweet dessert. Dried apples can be found in the dried fruit section of your supermarket.

9 X 13-INCH BAKING PAN / 24 SQUARES

2½ cups dried apples
2½ cups water or apple juice
1   teaspoon cinnamon
2   Tablespoons lemon juice

3   cups rolled oats
1   cup all-purpose flour
1   cup whole-wheat flour
¼   teaspoon salt
1   cup maple syrup (best with pure maple syrup)
     Nonfat cooking spray

Preheat oven to 350°F. Spray 9 x 13-inch pan with cooking spray. In a saucepan, bring first 4 ingredients to a boil. Simmer until apples are soft; adding more water if necessary. Purée in a blender until smooth. Set aside in a separate bowl.

In a large mixing bowl, stir together oats, flour, and salt. Add maple syrup and mix until well blended. Press ½ of the oatmeal mixture into prepared 9 x 13-inch pan. Spread apple purée to cover, then sprinkle with remaining oatmeal mixture. Bake at 350°F for about 35 minutes or until lightly browned on top.

Prep/cook time: 1 hour

NUTRITIONAL ANALYSIS PER SERVING:
Serving Size: 1 square

Calories:	116	Cholesterol:	0
Protein:	3 g	Fiber:	2 g
Carbohydrate:	25 g	Sodium:	25 mg
Fat:	1 g	Calcium	18 mg
		Iron	1 mg

Diabetic Exchanges: 1 starch, 1 fruit

Apple Crisp

Any type of apple works well in this recipe. It has about one-fourth the fat calories of a typical apple crisp.

8-INCH SQUARE BAKING DISH / 6 PORTIONS

4	large apples, peeled and sliced in wedges
½	cup all-purpose flour
½	cup rolled oats
½	cup brown sugar
¼	cup light margarine
1	teaspoon cinnamon
½	teaspoon nutmeg
	Nonfat cooking spray

Preheat oven to 375°F. Spray an 8-inch square baking dish with cooking spray. Place apple slices in the baking dish. In a small bowl, combine remaining ingredients until crumbly; sprinkle over apples. Bake at 375°F for 25 to 30 minutes or until apples are tender.

Prep/bake time: 1 hour

NUTRITIONAL ANALYSIS PER SERVING:
Serving Size: 1 portion

Calories:	180	Cholesterol:	0
Protein:	4 g	Fiber:	2 g
Carbohydrate:	36 g	Sodium:	100 mg
Fat:	4 g	Calcium	18 mg
		Iron	2 mg

Diabetic Exchanges: 2 starches

Blueberry Cobbler

Fresh blueberries, cherries, or peaches work well in this recipe.

4 CUSTARD CUPS / 4 PORTIONS

1   cup fresh blueberries
¼   cup light corn syrup

1   graham cracker, crushed
¼   cup all-purpose flour
2   Tablespoons sugar
¼   cup nonfat vanilla yogurt
2   egg whites (or ¼ cup nonfat egg substitute)
½   teaspoon baking powder
¼   teaspoon vanilla extract

Preheat oven to 350°F. In a small bowl, combine blueberries with corn syrup. Divide blueberry mixture evenly among 4 custard cups. In a separate bowl, combine remaining ingredients. Spoon batter over berry mixture.

Sprinkle with a teaspoon of sugar if desired. Bake at 350°F for 25 to 30 minutes or until topping is golden brown. Best when served warm.

Prep/bake time: 1 hour

NUTRITIONAL ANALYSIS PER SERVING:
Serving Size: 1 custard cup

Calories:	160	Cholesterol:	0
Protein:	3 g	Fiber:	1 g
Carbohydrate:	37 g	Sodium:	70 mg
Fat:	0	Calcium	26 mg
		Iron	1 mg

Diabetic Exchanges: 1 starch, 1 fruit

Winter Fruit Compote

This recipe can easily be doubled as it disappears fast!

8-INCH SQUARE BAKING DISH / 3 PORTIONS

1   large apple, unpeeled, cut in wedges
1   large pear, unpeeled, cut in wedges
1   Tablespoon fresh squeezed lemon juice
⅔   cup whole cranberries, cut in half*
1½ Tablespoons white flour
⅓   cup raisins
1   Tablespoon cornstarch
⅔   cup apple or grape juice
     Sprinkle of cinnamon

Preheat oven to 350°F. Place apple and pear wedges in an 8-inch square baking dish and toss with lemon juice. Add cranberries and flour; toss. Add raisins. Mix cornstarch with apple juice in a measuring cup until the cornstarch dissolves and pour over the fruit. Sprinkle with cinnamon.

Cover with foil and bake for approximately 45 minutes at 350°F. Place the 8-inch square baking dish onto a cookie sheet as the liquid can bubble over in the oven. Serve warm or at room temperature.

*If you wish, pop the cranberries open by heating them in a saucepan with a little of the juice.

Prep/bake time: 1 hour

NUTRITIONAL ANALYSIS PER SERVING:
Serving Size: 1 portion

Calories:	100	Cholesterol:	0
Protein:	1 g	Fiber:	4 g
Carbohydrate:	24 g	Sodium:	0
Fat:	0	Calcium	16 mg
		Iron	0

Diabetic Exchanges: 2 fruits

Fresh Fruit Smoothie

You can substitute any fruit you like for the strawberries.

3 CUPS / 2 SERVINGS

1	8-ounce carton nonfat vanilla yogurt
1	cup fresh strawberries
1	ripe banana
¼	cup orange juice
2-3	ice cubes

Place all ingredients in a blender or food processor. Cover and blend until smooth. Serve immediately. Garnish with a fresh strawberry, if desired.

Prep time: 5 minutes

NUTRITIONAL ANALYSIS PER SERVING:
Serving Size: 1½ cups

Calories:	150	Cholesterol:	0
Protein:	6 g	Fiber:	3 g
Carbohydrate:	34 g	Sodium:	70 mg
Fat:	0	Calcium	185 mg
		Iron	1 mg

Diabetic Exchanges: 1 fruit, 1 milk

Creamsicle Pie

This is a frozen dessert made to mimic a creamsicle on a stick. Make in an 8-inch pie plate or make individual pies in custard cups.

8-INCH PIE / 8 PIECES

1½ cups crushed graham cracker crumbs
(20 squares)
1 egg white
2 Tablespoons water

2 cups nonfat vanilla yogurt
¼ cup orange juice
⅓ cup sugar
1 Tablespoon orange-flavored liqueur, if desired
1 Tablespoon shaved orange rind, if desired

Preheat oven to 375°F. Crumb the crackers in a blender and place in bowl. Add the egg white and water; blend together until mixture is crumbly. Pat into an 8-inch glass pie plate. Bake the crust for 10 to 12 minutes at 375°F. Cool.

Combine remaining ingredients in a mixing bowl. Pour over cooled pie crust. Freeze and serve while still frozen.

Prep/bake time: 45 minutes

NUTRITIONAL ANALYSIS PER SERVING:
Serving Size: 1 piece

Calories:	100	Cholesterol:	0
Protein:	4 g	Fiber:	0
Carbohydrate:	18 g	Sodium:	110 mg
Fat:	1 g	Calcium	114 mg
		Iron	0

Diabetic Exchanges: 1 milk

Raspberry-Yogurt Pie

This easy-to-prepare pie makes a refreshing frozen dessert in warm weather.

9-INCH PIE / 8 PIECES

1½ cups crushed graham cracker crumbs
    (20 squares)
2   Tablespoons light margarine

1   12-ounce package frozen unsweetened
    raspberries
3   egg whites
½   cup sugar
1   8-ounce container nonfat vanilla yogurt

Preheat oven to 375°F. In a small bowl, melt the margarine and add crushed graham cracker crumbs; blend well. Press firmly into a 9-inch pie plate. Bake at 375°F for 10 minutes. Remove and cool.

In deep bowl, add berries and egg whites. Gradually add sugar. Beat with electric mixer until creamy. Gently fold in yogurt. Spread filling over graham cracker crust and freeze. Serve frozen.

Prep/bake time: 45 minutes

NUTRITIONAL ANALYSIS PER SERVING:
Serving Size: 1 piece

Calories:	165	Cholesterol:	0
Protein:	3 g	Fiber:	2 g
Carbohydrate:	31 g	Sodium:	90 mg
Fat:	3 g	Calcium	60 mg
		Iron	0

Diabetic Exchanges: 1 starch, 1 fruit

Sweet Potato Mini-Pies

Canned sweet potatoes work just as well as fresh.

6 CUSTARD CUPS

8	graham cracker squares, crushed into crumbs
1	egg white

1	cup cooked and mashed sweet potatoes
½	cup nonfat egg substitute
¼	cup molasses
¼	cup light corn syrup
½	cup skim milk
1	teaspoon vanilla extract
½	teaspoon cinnamon
	Nonfat cooking spray

Preheat oven to 375°F. Spray 6 custard cups with cooking spray. In a small bowl, mix the graham cracker crumbs with the egg white and press into the bottom of the 6 custard cups. Mix the cooled sweet potatoes with the remaining ingredients and divide evenly among the 6 cups. Place custard cups in a 9 x 13-inch baking pan filled with 1-inch of water. Place pan with filled custard cups in the center of the oven. Bake at 375°F for 45 minutes or until toothpick or knife comes out clean. Serve warm.

Prep/bake time: 1½ hours

NUTRITIONAL ANALYSIS PER SERVING:
Serving Size: 1 custard cup

Calories:	130	Cholesterol:	0
Protein:	4 g	Fiber:	1 g
Carbohydrate:	27 g	Sodium:	110 mg
Fat:	1 g	Calcium	83 mg
		Iron	2 mg

Diabetic Exchanges: 2 starches

Apple Mini-Pies

This recipe uses phyllo dough as the crust instead of pastry crust,
which reduces the fat content. If the phyllo is frozen, place in the refrigerator
for a few hours before using. Do not allow the phyllo dough to be exposed
to the open air until you are ready to coat and stuff the pies.

12 MINI-PIES

6	medium apples, peeled and sliced
¼	cup sugar
1	teaspoon cinnamon

6	sheets phyllo dough
2	Tablespoons olive oil
1	Tablespoon amaretto liqueur*
	(or light corn syrup)
	Nonfat cooking spray

Preheat oven to 375°F. Prepare apples; add cinnamon and sugar. Place in the microwave and cook until the apples are bendable (check every 30 seconds). Carefully lay out 2 sheets of phyllo dough on a cutting board. In a small bowl, combine the oil and liqueur. Wet a pastry brush with water and lightly brush the 2 sheets of phyllo dough, repeat this twice. Cut the dough evenly into quarters and place apple filling, about ¼ cup apple mixture, in the center of each quarter. Fold like you are wrapping a present—two opposite sides first, then the other opposite sides over each other. Place the four packages on a cookie sheet lightly sprayed with cooking spray. Repeat with 2 more sets of twin phyllo sheets to make 12 mini pies. Bake at 375°F for about 10 minutes or until edges turn golden brown.

*Orange flavored liqueur or rice syrup can be substituted for the amaretto liqueur.

Prep/bake time: 1 hour

NUTRITIONAL ANALYSIS PER SERVING:
Serving Size: 1 mini pie

Calories:	100	Cholesterol:	0
Protein:	1 g	Fiber:	1 g
Carbohydrate:	19 g	Sodium:	50 mg
Fat:	2 g	Calcium	4 mg
		Iron	0

Diabetic Exchanges: 1 starch, 1 fruit

Rice Pudding

This is an easy, satisfying recipe that children also enjoy. Top with a little crushed pineapple,if desired and serve warm or chilled.

2-QUART BAKING DISH / 6 PORTIONS

3	cups skim milk
⅓	cup white rice, uncooked
¼	cup sugar
½	teaspoon vanilla extract
⅛	teaspoon nutmeg
¼	teaspoon cinnamon
¼	cup raisins (optional)

Preheat oven to 325°F. In a 2-quart baking dish, combine all ingredients. Bake at 325°F for 1½ hours, stirring occasionally to break the film forming on top. You may need more or less time, depending on the type of bakeware, to get a desired creamy consistency. Serve warm or cold.

Prep/bake time: 1¾ hours

NUTRITIONAL ANALYSIS PER SERVING:
Serving Size: 1 portion

Calories:	130	Cholesterol:	0
Protein:	5 g	Fiber:	0
Carbohydrate:	28 g	Sodium:	65 mg
Fat:	0	Calcium	157 mg
		Iron	1 mg

Diabetic Exchanges: 1 starch, 1 milk

Deluxe Bread Pudding

This recipe makes a filling, high-protein dessert or snack.

9-INCH SQUARE BAKING DISH / 9 PORTIONS

4   slices whole-wheat bread (or white)
2   Tablespoons lowfat margarine
⅓   cup brown sugar
½   teaspoon cinnamon
⅓   cup raisins (if desired)

1   cup nonfat egg substitute
¼   cup granulated sugar
1   teaspoon vanilla
⅛   teaspoon salt
2½ cups skim milk
    Nonfat cooking spray

Preheat oven to 350°F. Spray a 9 x 9-inch glass baking dish with cooking spray. Toast bread slices lightly and spread with margarine. Sprinkle with brown sugar and cinnamon. Put two slices together to make 2 sandwiches. Remove crust. Cut each sandwich into 4 rectangles. Arrange the 8 rectangles in a single layer in the baking dish. Sprinkle with raisins.

In a bowl, blend together egg substitute, sugar, vanilla, and salt; then stir in milk. Slowly pour over toast. Place baking dish into larger pan filled with 1-inch of water. Bake at 350°F for 60 to 70 minutes or until knife inserted near center comes out clean. Serve warm or cold.

Prep/bake time: 1¾ hours

NUTRITIONAL ANALYSIS PER SERVING:			
Serving Size: 1 portion			
Calories:	140	Cholesterol:	0
Protein:	6 g	Fiber:	1 g
Carbohydrate:	25 g	Sodium:	210 mg
Fat:	2 g	Calcium	124 mg
		Iron	1 mg
Diabetic Exchanges: 1 fruit, 1 milk			

Indian Pudding

This cold-weather dessert can be served with or without a scoop of frozen nonfat vanilla yogurt.

8-INCH SQUARE BAKING DISH / 9 PORTIONS

4	cups 1% lowfat milk, divided
¾	cup cornmeal
⅔	cup molasses
1	Tablespoon oil
1	teaspoon cinnamon
¼	teaspoon ground ginger
½	cup nonfat egg substitute
	Nonfat cooking spray

Preheat oven to 325°F. Spray 8-inch square baking dish with cooking spray. In a large saucepan, combine 2 cups of milk and cornmeal. Heat on medium heat, stirring frequently, until the mixture thickens. Take the mixture off the heat and add the remaining 2 cups of milk and remaining ingredients. Pour into prepared baking dish.

Bake 1½ hours at 325°F. There will be a browned crust and the inside will be the consistency of bread pudding. Bake for less time if you prefer a softer consistency. Remove the crust before eating.

Prep/bake time: 2 hours

NUTRITIONAL ANALYSIS PER SERVING:
Serving Size: 1 portion

Calories:	160	Cholesterol:	0
Protein:	6 g	Fiber:	1 g
Carbohydrate:	30 g	Sodium:	90 mg
Fat:	2 g	Calcium	191 mg
		Iron	2 mg

Diabetic Exchanges: 1 starch, 1 milk

Island Banana Pudding

This is a slight variation of a traditional Filipino recipe. It's very sweet and has the consistency of bread pudding. I use 1% milk because it gives a desired custard-type consistency.

8-INCH SQUARE BAKING DISH / 9 PORTIONS

8	graham cracker squares, crushed into crumbs
2	Tablespoons light margarine, melted
2	large or 3 small ripe bananas
⅓	cup sugar
½	cup nonfat egg substitute
2	cups 1% lowfat milk
1	teaspoon vanilla extract
	Nonfat cooking spray

Preheat oven to 375°F. Spray 8-inch square baking dish with cooking spray. In a medium bowl, combine cracker crumbs and margarine. Slice half of the bananas along the bottom of the baking dish. Sprinkle ½ of the cracker crumbs over the bananas. Add another layer of sliced bananas, then remaining crumbs. In separate bowl, combine sugar, egg substitute, milk, and vanilla. Pour over banana-crumb layers. Bake at 375°F in center of oven for 40 to 45 minutes, until a knife inserted in center comes out clean. You may need to place a cookie sheet on the bottom rack to catch the liquid that bubbles over.

Prep/bake time: 1½ hours

NUTRITIONAL ANALYSIS PER SERVING:
Serving Size: 1 portion

Calories:	120	Cholesterol:	0
Protein:	4 g	Fiber:	1 g
Carbohydrate:	21 g	Sodium:	110 mg
Fat:	2 g	Calcium	76 mg
		Iron	1 mg

Diabetic Exchanges: 1 starch, 1 fruit

Amaretto Flan

*This is one of my favorite dessert recipes; a great way to keep fat intake
low and satisfy your sweet tooth.*

5 CUSTARD CUPS / 5 PORTIONS

¼   cup amaretto liqueur
¼   cup light corn syrup

1½ cups 1% lowfat milk
1   cup nonfat egg substitute
1   teaspoon almond extract
¼   cup light corn syrup

Preheat oven to 325°F. In a very small saucepan, combine liqueur and
¼ cup corn syrup. Heat for 4 to 5 minutes, stirring, until mixture starts
to caramelize and thicken. Distribute evenly into 5 custard cups.
You shouldn't need to use all of the syrup.

Cool custard cups in the refrigerator while you combine milk, egg
substitute, almond extract and ¼ cup corn syrup. Fill custard cups with
the milk mixture and place into a baking pan filled with 1-inch water. Place
baking pan in center of oven; bake at 325°F for about 1 hour or until a
knife inserted in the center comes out clean. Before serving, invert
custard cups on dessert plate.

Prep/cook time: 1½ hours

NUTRITIONAL ANALYSIS PER SERVING:
Serving Size: 1 custard cup

Calories:	140	Cholesterol:	0
Protein:	7 g	Fiber:	0
Carbohydrate:	27 g	Sodium:	140 mg
Fat:	1 g	Calcium	118 mg
		Iron	1 mg

Diabetic Exchanges: 1 starch, 1 milk

Apple Spice Cake

A light oil, such as canola or safflower, works well in this recipe.
Use regular or decaf coffee.

8-INCH SQUARE BAKING DISH / 12 PIECES

¼ cup vegetable oil
¼ cup black coffee
⅔ cup honey
2 small or 1 large apple, peeled and chopped
¼ cup nonfat egg substitute
½ cup applesauce

2 cups all-purpose flour
1 teaspoon cinnamon
¼ teaspoon ground cloves
1 Tablespoon baking powder
   Nonfat cooking spray

Preheat oven to 325°F. Spray 8-inch square baking dish with cooking spray. In mixing bowl, combine the first 6 ingredients. In separate bowl, combine next 4 dry ingredients. Add flour mixture to liquid mixture; blend together just long enough to mix evenly. Pour batter into 8-inch square baking dish. Bake at 325°F for 30 to 35 minutes or until a toothpick inserted in center comes out clean.

Prep/bake time: 50 minutes

NUTRITIONAL ANALYSIS PER SERVING:			
Serving Size: 1 piece			
Calories:	180	Cholesterol:	0
Protein:	4 g	Fiber:	3 g
Carbohydrate:	33 g	Sodium:	100 mg
Fat:	4 g	Calcium	12 mg
		Iron	1 mg

Diabetic Exchanges: 2 starches

Hawaiian Pineapple Turnovers

Turnovers you can indulge in without the saturated fat.

12 TURNOVERS

Filling:
1   cup canned crushed pineapple,
      drain and save juice
1   Tablespoon cornstarch
⅓   cup sugar

Pastry:
2   cups all-purpose flour
½   teaspoon salt
¼   cup safflower or canola oil
¼   cup skim milk
3   Tablespoons water
      Nonfat cooking spray

To make filling: Pour ⅔ cup drained pineapple juice into a small saucepan. Add cornstarch and sugar to the juice and heat, stirring frequently, until mixture thickens into a syrup. Add the drained pineapple.

To make pastry: Preheat oven to 425°F. Combine all pastry ingredients together, except the water. Add water to mixture, one tablespoon at a time. After mixing, pick up dough with your hands and work it until you get a pliable pastry dough. An additional tablespoon of water may be needed. Lightly flour a working surface and divide the dough into 4 portions. Roll out each portion very thin. Cut circles with a large cookie cutter or glass with a 3 to 3½-inch diameter, making 12 circles. *(continued on next page)*

NUTRITIONAL ANALYSIS PER SERVING:
Serving Size: 1 turnover

Calories:	150	Cholesterol:	0
Protein:	3 g	Fiber:	1 g
Carbohydrate:	24 g	Sodium:	90 mg
Fat:	4 g	Calcium	13 mg
		Iron	1 mg

Diabetic Exchanges: 1 starch, 1 fruit

To assemble: Place 1½ tablespoons of filling in lower half of each circle, keeping the edges dry. Flip top half of circle over filling and seal with a wet fork.

Place turnovers on a sheet sprayed with cooking spray. Trim uneven ends with a knife. Bake at 425°F for 12 to 15 minutes or until golden brown.

Prep/bake time: 1½ hours

Fruit Topping for Angel Food Cake

This is a satisfying alternative to whipped topping. Use a homemade or bakery-made angel food cake. Strawberries can be substituted for raspberries.

8 SERVINGS

1	10 or 12 ounce bag of frozen raspberries
⅔	cup evaporated skim milk
¼	cup brown sugar

Place fruit, milk, and sugar into blender and purée. Pour into a small sauce pan and heat until warm.

Divide the cake into 8 slices and pour topping over each slice.

Prep/cook time: 15 minutes

NUTRITIONAL ANALYSIS PER SERVING:			
Serving Size: ⅛ *of cake with* ⅓ *cup sauce*			
Calories:	90	Cholesterol:	0
Protein:	2 g	Fiber:	2 g
Carbohydrate:	20 g	Sodium:	80 mg
Fat:	0	Calcium	79 mg
		Iron	0

Diabetic Exchanges: 1 starch

Strawberry Couscous Cake

This no-bake cake is surprisingly simple and contains almost no fat.
You can find the couscous at any health food store or in the health food section
of your supermarket.

9 X 13-INCH BAKING PAN / 15 PORTIONS

Cake:
6   cups apple juice
3   cups couscous, uncooked
1   Tablespoon vanilla extract
¼   teaspoon salt

Fresh Strawberry Topping:
1   cup fresh or frozen strawberries
⅔   cup apple juice
1   Tablespoon cornstarch
½   teaspoon lemon juice
½   teaspoon vanilla extract

Strawberry Jam Topping:
1⅓ cups water
3   Tablespoons strawberry jam
1½ Tablespoons cornstarch

To make cake: In a large saucepan, combine apple juice, uncooked couscous, vanilla, and salt. Bring to a boil; cook on medium heat, stirring, until liquid is absorbed and couscous is very soft (10 minutes). Pour into a 9 x 13-inch baking pan. Top with either topping.

To make topping: In a small saucepan, combine all ingredients. Cook over medium heat, stirring constantly, until sauce thickens. Pour over cake. Refrigerate and serve cold. **Prep/bake time: 30 minutes**

NUTRITIONAL ANALYSIS PER SERVING:
Serving Size: 1 portion

Calories:	140	Cholesterol:	0
Protein:	3 g	Fiber:	1 g
Carbohydrate:	32 g	Sodium:	420 mg
Fat:	0	Calcium	15 mg
		Iron	1 mg

Diabetic Exchanges: 1 starch, 1 fruit

Suggestions for Further Reading

Duyff, Roberta Laison.*The ADA's Complete Food and Nutrition Guide*. Chronimed Press, 1996.

Hess, Mary Abbott. *Pocket Supermarket Guide*. The American Dietetic Association, eds. Chronimed Press, 1996.

Katzen, Mollie. *Moosewood Cookbook, Revised edition*. Berkeley, CA: Ten Speed Press, 1992.

Katzen, Mollie. *Moosewood Restaurant Cooks at Home*. Simon & Schuster, 1994.

Magida, Phyllis & Spitler, Sue. *Skinny Vegetarian Entrées*. Surrey Books, 1995.

Moore Zappé, Frances. *Diet For a Small Planet*, Revised edition. New York: Balantine Press, 1991.

Ornish, Dean. *Dr. Dean Ornish's Program For Reversing Heart Disease*. New York: Balantine Books, 1990.

Ornish, Dean. *Eat More, Weigh Less*. New York: HarperCollins Publishers, Inc., 1993.

Ornish, Dean. *Everyday Cooking with Dr. Dean Ornish*. New York: HarperCollins Publishers, Inc., 1996.

Roth, Geneen. *Feeding the Hungry Heart*. New York: Penguin Books, 1982.

TerMeer, Mary and Jamie Gates Galeana. *Vegetarian Cooking For Healthy Living*. Mankato, MN: Appletree Press, Inc., 1997.

Stevens, R. and Stevens, J., eds. *U.S. 1997 Soy Foods Directory*. Indiana Soybean Development Council, 1997. (800) 301-3153.

Vegetarian Journal's Guide to Natural Foods Restaurants in the U.S. and Canada, Avery Publishing Group.

Web Sites for the Vegetarian

There are many ways to access information about vegetarian nutrition and cuisine on the internet. Here are a few web sites that you may want to visit:

1. WWW.EATRIGHT.ORG
This is the American Dietetic Association web site. It provides general nutritional information for the public. Try clicking on the nutrition resources or hot topics.

2. http://navigator.tufts.edu
This nutrition navigator provides a rating system and description of many nutrition web sites and contains links to those sites. For example, click on health professionals, then vegetarian resource group for their web site. You can find the American Heart Association web site by clicking on **special dietary**.

3. WWW.VEGWEB.COM
This is a commercial web site with recipes, book suggestions and a chat line.

4. WWW.NAL.USDA.GOV/FNIC
Provides all kinds of nutrition resources and publications from the USDA. Receive detailed 44-page brochure entitled, "Nutrition and Your Health: Dietary Guidelines for Americans."

5. Do a search with your net search in your internet program. For example, you could type in the words VEGETARIAN RECIPES in the net search blank box.

References

1. Bakhit, R.., et al. "Intake of 25 gms of soy protein with or without soybean fiber alters plasma lipids in men with elevated chol." *J Nutr.* 1994, Vol 124:213-222.

2. Boushey, C. J., Beresford, S.A., "A quantitative assessment of plasma homocysteine as a risk factor for vascular disease." *JAMA. 1995,* 274:1049.

3. Brestrick M., Claus J., Blumchen G., "Lactovegetarian diet: effect on changes in body wt, lipid status, fibrinogen and lipoprotein (a) in cardiovascular patients during inpatient rehabilitation treatment." *Z Kardiol.* 1996, 85:418-427.

4. Caggiula, A.W., Watson, J.E., "Characteristics assoc with compliance to cholesterol-lowering eating patterns." *Patient Educ Counseling.* 1992, 191:33-41.

5. Colditz, G., Wolf, A., "Social and economical effects of body weight in the United States." *Am J Clin Nutr,* 1996, 63:466s-469s.

6. Goor, R., and Goor, N., *Eater's Choice.* 1989, Houghton-Mifflin Press, New York, NY.

7. Gupta, R.,"Lifestyle risk factors and coronary heart disease prevalence in Indian men." *J Assoc Physicians India.* 1996, 44:689-793.

8. Hstmark A.T., Lystad E., Vellar D.D., Hovi K., Berg J.E., "Reduced plasmafibrinogen, serum peroxides, lipids, and apolipoproteins after a 3-week vegetarian diet." *Plant Foods Human Nutr.* 1993, 43:55-61.

9. Jacob, R.A., Burri, B.J., "Oxidative damage and defense." *Am J Clin Nutr.* 1996, 63:985s-990s.

10. Jacob, R.A., Wu, N.M., Henning, S.M., "Homocysteine increases as folate decreases in plasma of healthy men during short-term dietary folate and methyl group restriction." *J Nutr.* 1994, 124:1072.

11. Janelle, K.C., Barr, S.I., "Nutrient intakes and eating behavior scores of vegetarian and non-vegetarian women." *J Am Diet Assoc.*1995, 95:180-189.

12. Kanazawa, T., et al, "Anti-atherogenicity of Soybean Protein." *Annals NY Acad Sci. 1993,* 672:202-214.

13. Kang, S.S., Wong, P.W., Norusis, M., "Homocysteinemia due to folate deficiency." *Metabolism.* 1987, 36:458.

14. Kushi, L.H., Samonds, K.W., Lacey, J.M., Brown, P.T., "The association of dietary fat with serum cholesterol in vegetarians: the effect of dietary assessment on the correlation coefficient." *Am J Epidemiol.* 1988, 128:1054-64.

15. Lynch, S.R., Beard, J.L., Dassenko, S.A., Cook, J.D., "Iron absorption from legumes in humans." *Am J Clin Nutr.* 1984, 40:42-47.

16. Matsuo, M., Hitomi, E., "Suppression of plasma cholesterol elevation by okara tempe in rats." *Biosci Biotech Biochem.* 1993, 57:1188-1190.

17. "Meat—Can We Live Without It?" *World Health Forum. 1991,* 12:251-60; discussion 260-83.

18. Melby, C.L., Toohey, M.L., and Cebrick, J., "Blood pressure and blood lipids among vegetarian, semi-vegetarian, and non-vegetarian African Americans." *Am J Clin Nutr.* 1994, 59:103-109.

19. Mellin, L., Croughan, M., Dickey, L., "The solution method: 2 year trends in weight, blood pressure, exercise, depression, and functioning of adults trained in development skills." *J Am Diet Assoc.* 1997, 97:1133-1138.

20. Messina, M.J., Messina, V.L., *The dietitian's guide to vegetarian diets: issues and applications.* 1996, Aspen Publishers, Gaithersburg, MD.

21. Morrison, H.I., Schaubel, D., "Serum folate and risk of fatal coronary disease." *JAMA.* 1996, 275:1893.

22. Nelson, L. and Tucker, L., "Diet Composition related to body fat in a multivariate study of 203 men." *J Am Diet Assoc.* 1996, 96:771-777.

23. Nieman, D.C., et al, "Dietary status of 7th Day Adventist vegetarian and non-vegetarian women." *J Am Diet Assoc.* 1989, 89:1763-1769.

24. Ornish, D., *Dr. Dean Ornish's Program for Reversing Heart Disease.* 1990, Ballantine Books, New York, NY.

25. Oster, G., Thompson, D., "Estimated effects of reducing dietary saturated fat intake on the incidence and costs of coronary heart disease." *J Am Diet Assoc.* 1996, 96:127-131.

26. Phinney, S.D., Odin, R.S., Johnson, S.B., Homan, R.T., "Reduced arachidonatein serum phospholipids and cholesteryl esters associated with vegetarian diets in humans." *Am J Clin Nutr.* 1990, 51:385-92.

27. Potter, S.M., et al, "Depression of plasma cholesterol in men by consumption of baked products containing soy protein." *Am J Clin Nutr.* 1993, 58:501-506.

28. Resnicow, et al, "Diet and serum lipids in vegan vegetarians: A model for risk reduction." *J Am Diet Assoc.* 1991, 91:447-53.

29. Russell, B., Harris, B., Huster, G., Sprecher, D., "Effect of premature myocardial infarction in men on the eating habits of spouses and offspring." *J Am Diet Assoc.* 1994, 94:859-864.

30. Saltzer, E.B., " The weight locus of control (WLOC) scale: A specific measure for obesity research." *J Pers Asses.*1982, 46:620-628.

31. Schlundt, D. G., Rea, M.R., Kline, S.S., and Pichert, J.W., "Situational obstacles to dietary adherence for adults with diabetes." *J Am Diet Assoc.* 1994, 94:874-879.

32. Shrapnel, W.S., Calvert, G.D., Nestel, P.J., Truswell, A.S., "Diet and coronary heart disease." *Med J Aust.* 1992, 156:S9-16.

33. Steinmetz, K.A., Potter, J.D., "Vegetables, fruit, and cancer." *Cancer Causes Control.* 1991, 1:427-442.

34. Vogel, R., Corretti, M., Plotnick, G., "Effect of a single high fat meal on endothelial function in healthy subjects." *Am J Cardiol.* 1997, 79:350-354.

35. Young, V. R., "Soy protein in relation to human protein and amino acid nutrition." *J Am Diet Assoc.* 1991, 91:828-835.

Appendix A:
American Heart Association Eating Plan for Healthy Americans[1]

Apply these eight guidelines to total calories eaten over several days, such as a week:

❖ Total fat intake should be no more than 30% of total calories.

❖ Saturated fatty acid intake should be 8-10% of total calories.

❖ Polyunsaturated fatty acid intake should be up to 10% of total calories.

❖ Monounsaturated fatty acids make up 15% of total calories.

❖ Cholesterol intake should be less than 300 milligrams per day.

❖ Sodium intake should be less than 2400 milligrams per day, which is about 6000 milligrams (6 grams) of sodium chloride (salt).

❖ Carbohydrate intake should make up 55-60% or more of calories, with emphasis on increasing sources of complex carbohydrates.

❖ Total calories should be adjusted to achieve and maintain a healthy body weight.

Exchange Lists for Meal Planning[2]

Please note that the exchanges listed in *Vegetarian Homestyle Cooking* will give milk exchanges as "milk" because recipes contain only skim or 1% milk. Meat exchanges are given as "protein" noting that most recipes call for little or no added fat. When a higher fat protein is given, the added fat will appear as a "fat" exchange.

	Carbohydrate (grams)	Protein (grams)	Fat (grams)	Calories
CARBOHYDRATE GROUP				
Starch	15	3	<1	80
Fruit	15	-	-	60
Milk				
skim	12	8	0-3	90
lowfat (2%)	12	8	5	120
Whole	12	8	8	150
Other carbo	15	varies	varies	varies
Vegetables	5	2	-	25
MEAT AND MEAT SUBSTITUTE GROUP				
Very lean	-	7	0-1	35
Lean	-	7	3	55
Medium fat	-	7	5	75
High fat	-	7	8	100
FAT GROUP	-	-	5	45

Appendix B: The Vegetarian Food Guide Pyramid

A Daily Guide to Food Choices

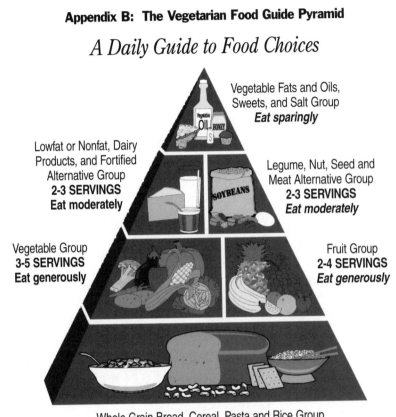

Vegetable Fats and Oils, Sweets, and Salt Group
Eat sparingly

Lowfat or Nonfat, Dairy Products, and Fortified Alternative Group
2-3 SERVINGS
Eat moderately

Legume, Nut, Seed and Meat Alternative Group
2-3 SERVINGS
Eat moderately

Vegetable Group
3-5 SERVINGS
Eat generously

Fruit Group
2-4 SERVINGS
Eat generously

Whole Grain Bread, Cereal, Pasta and Rice Group
6-11 SERVINGS—*Eat liberally*

© 1994 The Health Connection. The Vegetarian Food Guide Pyramid is available as a poster and as handouts from the Health Connection. 1-800-548-8700. Used with permission.

Dietary Guidelines for Americans

Use these seven guidelines together as you choose a healthful vegetarian diet.

❖ Eat a variety of foods.

❖ Balance the food you eat with physical activity—maintain or improve your weight.

❖ Choose a diet with plenty of grain products, vegetables, and fruits.

❖ Choose a diet low in fat, saturated fat, and cholesterol.

❖ Choose a diet moderate in sugars.

❖ Choose a diet moderate in salt and sodium.

❖ If you drink alcoholic beverages, do so in moderation.

©1995 U.S. Dept. of Agriculture and U.S. Dept. of Health & Human Services. "Nutrition and Your Health: Dietary Guidelines For Americans." Used with permission. Available by writing to Center for Nutrition Policy and Promotions; 1120 20 St. NW, Suite 200 North Lobby; Washington, DC 20036

Appendix C: First Week of Sample Menus

DAY 1

Breakfast
high fiber cold cereal
6 ounces skim milk
1 banana
decaf coffee
with 2 tablespoons skim milk

Lunch
bowl of minestrone soup
2 slices whole grain bread
2 teaspoons jam or jelly
diet drink or water

Snack
3 cups popcorn
(popped with 1 teaspoon oil)
12 ounces fruit juice

Supper
sub-gum chow mein
1 cup of cooked rice
1 cup pineapple chunks
herbal tea

Snack
1/2 cup spicy bean dip
pita bread

Calories: 1577
Protein: 52 g
Carbohydrate: 302 g
Fat: 23 g
Cholesterol: 3 mg
% calories/fat: 13 %
Fiber: 27 g
Sodium: 1838 mg

DAY 2

Breakfast
English muffin
2 teaspoons jelly
8 ounces orange juice
decaf coffee
with 2 tablespoons skim milk

Lunch
1 cup mexican corn
& bean salad over corn tortilla,
cut in bite-size pieces
bunch of grapes (about 20)
diet drink or water

Snack
1/2 cup 1% lowfat cottage
cheese, mixed with 1 teaspoon
sweet green relish
6 lowfat soda crackers

Supper
2 cups spaghetti
with lowfat pasta sauce
tossed salad with 2 tablespoons
light salad dressing
diet drink or water

Snack
fresh fruit or fruit pop

Calories: 1443
Protein: 55 g
Carbohydrate: 279 g
Fat: 15 g
Cholesterol: 7 mg
% calories/fat: 10 %
Fiber: 25 g
Sodium: 1982

DAY 3

Breakfast
2 Bran muffins with applesauce
1/4 large cantaloupe
decaf coffee
with 2 tablespoons skim milk

Lunch
leftover minestrone soup (day 1)
tossed salad
with 2 tablespoons fat-free
salad dressing
8 ounces skim milk

Snack
mocha brownie
6 ounces cranberry juice on ice

Supper
Chinese vegetables
with marinated tofu
boiled rice, 1 cup
herbal tea
1 cup pineapple chunks

Snack
3 graham crackers
sugar free iced herbal tea

Calories: 1415
Protein: 48 g
Carbohydrate: 268 g
Cholesterol: 6 mg
Fat: 23 g
% calories/fat: 15 %
Fiber: 25 g
Sodium: 1632 mg

DAY 4

Breakfast
2 lowfat toaster waffles
1/4 cup light maple syrup
1 banana
decaf coffee
with 2 tablespoons skim milk

Lunch
1/2 cup hummus spread in
1/2 pita bread
1/4 cantaloupe
diet drink or water

Snack
mocha brownie (day 3)
8 ounces skim milk

Supper
pasta primavera, large portion
diet drink or water

Snack
3 graham crackers
herbal tea

Calories: 1639
Protein: 54 g
Carbohydrate: 302 g
Cholesterol: 6 mg
Fat: 20 g
% calories/fat: 11 %
Fiber: 28 g
Sodium: 1655 mg

DAY 5

Breakfast
High fiber cereal
with 6 ounces skim milk
1 banana
decaf coffee
with 2 tablespoons skim milk

Lunch
Portuguese bean soup
3 breadsticks
apple
diet drink or water

Snack
bran muffin with applesauce
(day 3)
herbal tea or water

Supper
Home made pizza
salad
with fat-free Italian dressing
herbal tea

Snack
1 cup rice pudding

Calories: 1146
Protein: 42 g
Carbohydrate: 226 g
Cholesterol: 16 mg
Fat: 11 g
% calories/fat: 9 %
Fiber: 23 g
Sodium: 2305 mg

DAY 6

Breakfast
English muffin
2 teaspoons jelly
8 ounces orange juice
decaf coffee
with 2 tablespoons skim milk

Lunch
Spinach salad
2 tablespoons light
salad dressing
fat-free fruit yogurt
diet drink or water

Snack
fresh fruit or fruit pop
3 graham crackers

Supper
stir-fried rice delux
diet drink or water

Snack
1 raisin bagel
with 1 tablespoon apple butter

Calories: 1317
Protein: 44 g
Carbohydrate: 246 g
Cholesterol: 4 mg
Fat: 16 g
% calories/fat: 11 %
Fiber: 16 g
Sodium: 2047 mg

DAY 7

Breakfast
raisin bagel (day 6)
1 Tablespoon apple butter
8 ounces orange juice
decaf coffee
with 2 tablespoons skim milk

Lunch
Leftover pizza (day 5)
tossed salad with
2 tablespoons light salad
dressing
8 ounces skim milk

Snack
Leftover rice pudding (day 5)

Supper
pad-thai
1 cup pineapple chunks
diet drink or water

Snack
3 fig newtons or brownie (day 3)
herbal tea or decaf coffee

Calories: 1494
Protein: 48 g
Carbohydrate: 282 g
Cholesterol: 12 mg
Fat: 23 g
% calories/fat: 14 %
Fiber: 14 g
Sodium: 1758 mg

NOTE: Underlined recipes can be found in *Vegetarian Homestyle Cooking.*

DAY 8

Breakfast
raisin bagel with (day 6)
1 tablespoon apple butter
decaf coffee
with 2 tablespoons skim milk

Lunch
Soyburger, on hamburger roll
2 teaspoons vegetable oil
for cooking
1 tablespoon catsup
2 dill pickle spears
diet drink or water

Snack
banana
8 ounces skim milk

Supper
Spanish beans and rice
tossed salad with
2 tablespoons light dressing
diet drink or water

Snack
apple spice cake
herbal tea

Calories: 1342
Protein: 53 g
Carbohydrate: 238 g
Cholesterol: 5 mg
Fat: 19 g
% calories/fat: 13 %
Fiber: 20 g
Sodium: 2149 mg

DAY 9

Breakfast
fat-free toaster waffles, 2
2 tablespoons light syrup
8 ounces orange juice
decaf coffee
with 2 tablespoons skim milk

Lunch
hummus spread (day 4)
with pita bread
apple or banana
diet drink or water

Snack
2 fig newtons
herbal tea or water

Supper
bean burrito
2 tortillas
with chopped fresh tomato
boiled rice, 1 cup
1 glass beer (or wine) *optional*

Snack
amaretto flan

Calories: 1606
Protein: 46 g
Carbohydrate: 308 g
Cholesterol: 5 mg
Fat: 15 g
% calories/fat: 8 %
Fiber: 24 g
Sodium: 1770 mg

DAY 10

Breakfast
high fiber cereal
with 6 ounces skim milk
banana
decaf coffee
with 2 tablespoons skim milk

Lunch
leftover bean burrito (day 9)
with 1 cup rice
diet drink or water
leftover amaretto flan (day 9)

Supper
vegetable ring
tossed salad
with 2 tablespoons light dressing
herbal tea or water

Snack
6 lowfat crackers
fresh fruit
water or diet drink

Calories: 1612
Protein: 54 g
Carbohydrate: 305 g
Cholesterol: 9 mg
Fat: 23 g
% calories/fat: 13 %
Fiber: 26 g
Sodium: 2287 mg

DAY 11

Breakfast
English muffin
1 tablespoon orange
marmalade or jelly
8 ounces orange juice
decaf coffee
with 2 tablespoons skim milk

Lunch
soyburger on a hamburger roll
1 tablespoon catsup
tossed salad with
2 tablespoons fat-free dressing
diet drink or water
2 dill pickle spears

Snack
apple spice cake (day 8)
water

Supper
pasta fagioli
2 slices wheat bread
2 teaspoons light margarine
8 ounces skim milk

Snack
3 cups popcorn
1 teaspoon oil (for popping)
herbal tea or water

Calories: 1395
Protein: 61 g
Carbohydrate: 234 g
Cholesterol: 5 mg
Fat: 24 g
% calories/fat: 16 %
Fiber: 26 g
Sodium: 2766 mg

DAY 12

Breakfast
pumpkin muffin
8 ounces orange juice
decaf coffee
with 2 tablespoons skim milk

Lunch
leftover pasta fagioli (day 11)
oyster crackers (about 25)
8 ounces skim milk

Snack
fresh fruit

Supper
mixed vegetable curry
1 cup rice
diet drink or water

Snack
frozen fruit pop or
Italian ice
rice crackers (3) with jelly

Calories: 1494
Protein: 49 g
Carbohydrate: 288 g
Cholesterol: 6 mg
Fat: 17 g
% calories/fat: 10 %
Fiber: 17 g
Sodium: 1225 mg

DAY 13

Breakfast
leftover pumpkin muffin (day 12)
1/2 grapefruit
decaf coffee
with 2 tablespoons skim milk

Lunch
veggie-pita sandwich
apple or pear
diet drink or water

Snack
leftover apple spice cake (day 8)

Supper
zucchini lasagna
tossed salad
2 tablespoons lowfat dressing
8 ounces skim milk

Snack
fat-free fruit yogurt (1 cup)
herbal tea

Calories: 1180
Protein: 61 g
Carbohydrate: 189 g
Cholesterol: 8 mg
Fat: 18 g
% calories/fat: 13 %
Fiber: 19 g
Sodium: 2077 mg

DAY 14

Breakfast
2 slices french toast with
Eggbeaters® and skim milk
2 tablespoons light syrup
decaf coffee
with 2 tablespoons skim milk

Lunch
leftover zucchini lasagna
(day 13)
diet drink or water
fresh fruit

Snack
fig newtons (3)
8 ounces skim milk

Supper
Boston baked beans
cornbread or corn muffin
tossed salad
2 tablespoons low-cal dressing
diet drink or water

Snack
fat-free fruit yogurt

Calories: 1315
Protein: 64 g
Carbohydrate: 218 g
Cholesterol: 9 mg
Fat: 22 g
% calories/fat: 15 %
Fiber: 19 g
Sodium: 2448 mg

NOTE: Underlined recipes can be found in *Vegetarian Homestyle Cooking.*

Appendix D: Recommended Foods for a Lowfat Vegetarian Plan

	RECOMMENDED	RESTRICTED
PROTEIN GROUP	soy products, including tofu, tempeh, soy cheese TVP,® soy flour, soy milk all beans and dried peas vegetable protein substitute (sea vegetables) seitan (wheat protein) pasta with added casein egg whites/egg substitutes nuts and seeds, in moderate amounts	all meat, poultry fish pasta with eggs (i.e., egg noodles) egg yolks
DAIRY GROUP	skim or 1% milk, lowfat or nonfat yogurt nonfat cottage cheese lowfat or nonfat cheese	all other dairy
STARCH GROUP	all plain breads all cereals lowfat crackers (0-1 gm fat/serving) rice, any kind potatoes oats, oatmeal barley couscous dry pasta lowfat quick breads	high-fat crackers fried rice chips french fries high-fat quick breads
FRUIT GROUP	all fresh fruit canned fruit fruit juice fruit pops	
VEGETABLE GROUP	all plain, fresh and frozen vegetables	vegetables with cream sauce, margarine, or butter
FATS/OILS GROUP	small amounts of vegetable oil (i.e. canola, olive, safflower, soybean, or corn) lowfat margarine lowfat salad dressing	recommend no more than 1 Tablespoon of fat/day olives avocado all other fats
SWEETS GROUP	lowfat cookies lowfat cakes lowfat pies nonfat or lowfat frozen desserts hard candies gumdrops marshmallows	all pastries donuts high-fat cakes, cookies full-fat frozen desserts high-fat candies (i.e., chocolates)

Appendix E: How to Read a Food Label

Many Americans are now concerned with the over-consumption rather than the lack of nutrients; specifically the calories, fat, sugar, cholesterol and sodium content of foods. The current food labels specified by government regulation in 1993, reflect this and make it easier to focus on what you want to know. A sample label is listed below.

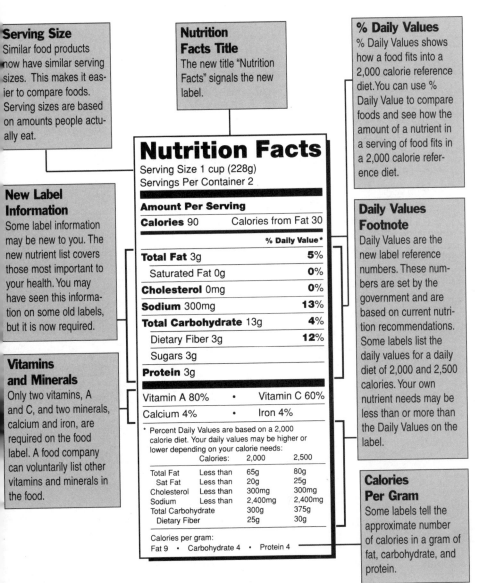

Serving Size
Similar food products now have similar serving sizes. This makes it easier to compare foods. Serving sizes are based on amounts people actually eat.

Nutrition Facts Title
The new title "Nutrition Facts" signals the new label.

% Daily Values
% Daily Values shows how a food fits into a 2,000 calorie reference diet. You can use % Daily Value to compare foods and see how the amount of a nutrient in a serving of food fits in a 2,000 calorie reference diet.

New Label Information
Some label information may be new to you. The new nutrient list covers those most important to your health. You may have seen this information on some old labels, but it is now required.

Daily Values Footnote
Daily Values are the new label reference numbers. These numbers are set by the government and are based on current nutrition recommendations. Some labels list the daily values for a daily diet of 2,000 and 2,500 calories. Your own nutrient needs may be less than or more than the Daily Values on the label.

Vitamins and Minerals
Only two vitamins, A and C, and two minerals, calcium and iron, are required on the food label. A food company can voluntarily list other vitamins and minerals in the food.

Calories Per Gram
Some labels tell the approximate number of calories in a gram of fat, carbohydrate, and protein.

Nutrition Facts

Serving Size 1 cup (228g)
Servings Per Container 2

Amount Per Serving

Calories 90   Calories from Fat 30

	% Daily Value*
Total Fat 3g	**5%**
Saturated Fat 0g	**0%**
Cholesterol 0mg	**0%**
Sodium 300mg	**13%**
Total Carbohydrate 13g	**4%**
Dietary Fiber 3g	**12%**
Sugars 3g	
Protein 3g	

Vitamin A 80%	•	Vitamin C 60%
Calcium 4%	•	Iron 4%

* Percent Daily Values are based on a 2,000 calorie diet. Your daily values may be higher or lower depending on your calorie needs:

		Calories:	2,000	2,500
Total Fat	Less than		65g	80g
Sat Fat	Less than		20g	25g
Cholesterol	Less than		300mg	300mg
Sodium	Less than		2,400mg	2,400mg
Total Carbohydrate			300g	375g
Dietary Fiber			25g	30g

Calories per gram:
Fat 9 • Carbohydrate 4 • Protein 4

Appendix F: Blending Herbs and Spices

If you have a few favorite combinations of herbs and spices, you may want to blend them in larger quantities to save cooking time. Make sure the herbs are dried and the jar is clean if you want to store them in an air-tight jar for a long time. You can, of course, omit any one of the herbs and spices or add more of your favorite one.

New Orleans cajun blend:
1 Tablespoon garlic powder
1 Tablespoon paprika
1 Tablespoon onion powder
1 teaspoon black pepper
1 Tablespoon thyme
1 teaspoon cayenne pepper
2 Tablespoons salt
2 teaspoons oregano

Curry powder:
2 teaspoons cloves, ground
2 teaspoons cinnamon
1 Tablespoon coriander
1 1/2 Tablespoons turmeric
1 teaspoon black pepper
1 teaspoon cayenne pepper
2 teaspoons cumin seed,ground
bay leaf *(optional)*

Spice blend to mimic salt:
2 Tablespoons dried basil
1 Tablespoon lemon rind (dry)
1 Tablespoon ground coriander
2 teaspoons black pepper

French blend:
1 Tablespoon thyme
1 Tablespoon marjoram
1 Tablespoon dry mustard
1/2 Tablespoon savory
1/2 Tablespoon black pepper
bay leaf

Italian blend:
2 Tablespoons parsley
2 teaspoons oregano
1 Tablespoon basil
1 teaspoon black pepper

Directions for all spice blends: Blend well and store in a tight-lid jar.

To make a "bouquet garni:" Add any herb/spice blend to a square of cheesecloth, folded to double layer strength. Tie the ends to make a bag with some string. Drop the bag into a soup or stew while cooking.

Hint: Herbs and spices blend well with a little oil. In many recipes quickly add a teaspoon of prepared spice blend while sautéing the garlic in olive oil.

Tip: Dried herbs should still have a strong aroma or they will need to be replaced.

Appendix G: Tips for Eating Out

I admit that finding a variety of lowfat vegetarian selections at local restaurants may not be easy. But fortunately, the choices are improving in many locations with increased interest in lowfat eating. This is because restaurants, like supermarkets, are consumer driven. In other words, if we request lowfat vegetarian items, restaurants will offer more of these items. Some restaurants display a red heart symbol next to the menu item, denoting that it is low in saturated fat and less than 30% of the calories come from fat. A few restaurants now have selections under a vegetarian heading.

In general, if you're looking for a variety of vegetarian items, start in ethnic restaurants from countries that don't eat much meat. These are Chinese, Japanese, Thai, Indian, Middle Eastern, or Mexican. Keep in mind that the Americanized versions of many ethnic entrées are higher in fat. So, the more authentic, the better.

The following specific guidelines might help you through the maze of restaurant choices:

❖ Enjoy a glass of wine or beer if you like, but remember these calories count as well. Alcohol is burned like a fat in the liver and a large amount of alcohol will slow down your metabolism.

❖ When attending a banquet or dinner party, eat smaller portions of the fattening items; serve yourself larger portions of bread, potato, salad, and fruit.

❖ Study the menu and don't be hesitant to ask the waiter how the dishes are prepared. Remember that you're paying for this food and restaurant owners want your repeat business.

❖ If others are ordering appetizers, choose a fresh fruit cup or broth-based soup. Minestrone or tomato soup is a good option.

❖ If there are no vegetarian entrées, try combining an appetizer with a salad or soup. There are usually pasta dishes that can be ordered without the meatsauce.

❖ In an Italian restaurant, you may want to try a pasta with Marinara or other meatless, red sauce. Avoid cream sauces.

❖ The salad bar may be a good option, but watch out for the creamy dressings, bacon, cheese, and eggs. Choose a vinaigrette-type dressing, if possible.

❖ The portions in most restaurants are larger than what the average person could comfortably eat. Therefore, try to avoid cleaning the plate after you're full. Unfortunately, we do not store excess protein in our bodies, so all calories eaten in excess will be stored as body fat.

❖ If you do over-consume foods with a high-fat content, forgive yourself and try to eat lighter at the next few meals. Feelings of guilt can sabotage your intent to eat healthier and to maintain your lowfat vegetarian plan.

Index

Vegetarian Homestyle Cooking

A Guide to Heart-Healthy Lowfat Eating
By Jeanne Tiberio, MS, RD.
A culturally-diverse collection of 175 mouth-watering recipes abounding with wholesome, heart-healthy dishes. 256 pages, Softcover.

$15.95 each: Send me _____ at $_____ .

ooking ala Heart

ore than 100,000 copies in print. Its recipes are always ailed as original, delicious and easy to make. Selected by e editors of Harvard Medical School Health Letter. Over 0 recipes! 456 pages, Softcover.

19.95 each: Send me_____at $_____ .

lealthy Mexican Cooking

40 authentic low-fat recipes for delicious, traditional lexican foods. Few ingredients, practical preparations and oderate to low calories. Diabetic exchanges and full nutri- nt analysis. 256 pages, Softcover.
vailable in **English or Spanish** Language Edition

15.95 each: Send me_____at $_____ .

iifts of the Heart

elightful recipes and gift ideas from Fudge Sauce to arbecue Sauce, Cookies and Snacks, even Soups and reads. Cute addition to a gift basket, perfect as a thank you r forget-me-not. 64 pages, Softcover.

8.50 each: Send me_____at $_____ .

)iabetic Goodie Book

)ver 190 recipes of desserts and baked goodies. ach formulated with small amounts of sugar or none at all. lo artificial sweeteners used. Includes carbohydrate choices, xchanges and nutrient analysis. 256 pages, Softcover.

15.95 each: Send me_____at $_____ .

"Naturally Good" Linen Notecards

Original, detailed pencil drawings create a nostalgic mood and emotion as they gracefully illustrate healthy food choices. Eight cards and envelopes to a set. Series I & II printed in green; Series III in brown. Blank inside.
Series I: Fruits & Vegetables
(apples, pears, asparagus, tomato/onion)
Series II: Fruits & Vegetables
(watermelon, strawberries, squash, and basket)
Series III: Whole Grains
(wheat bundle, muffins, loaf w/pitcher and breads)
$5.95 each, 2 sets for $10.00, 3 sets for $14.50
Send me _____ at $_____ .

The Essential Arthritis Cookbook

Kitchen Basics for People with Arthritis, Fibromyalgia and Other Chronic Pain and Fatigue. Excellent nutrition informa- tion, medication tables, photos and more. 120 low-fat recipes that save time and energy! 288 pages, Hardcover.

$24.95 each: Send me_____at $_____ .

What's For Breakfast?

The easiest way to stop cheating yourself out of a good breakfast. Over 100 recipes, easy and delicious. Super Quick, Quick and Worth the Effort. Sound nutrition and Pro-Carb Connection! 288 pages, Softcover.

$13.95 each: Send me_____at $_____ .

Vegetarian Cooking for Healthy Living

Over 130 creative, easy-to-follow recipes that are ultra low- fat and follow the heart reversal guidelines advocated by Dean Ornish, M.D. Full nutrient analysis. 262 pages, Softcover.

$17.95 each: Send me_____at $_____ .

SHIPPING INFORMATION: Add $4.00 for one book, $5.00/2 books, $6.00/3 books, $7.00/4-6 books $_____
(Minnesota residents must add sales tax) 6.5% tax $_____
TOTAL ENCLOSED $_____

Circle Method of Payment: **Check   Visa   MasterCard**

Card Number _____ Expiration Date_____

Name_____

P.O. Box and/or Street

Address_____

_____

City, State and Zip Code_____

MAIL TO: **Appletree Press, Inc.**   Toll-free: **1-800-322-5679**
Suite 125   Fax: (507) 345-3002
151 Good Counsel Drive   Phone: (507) 345-4848
Mankato, MN 56001